Also by Laurence Stapleton

Some Poets and Their Resources (1995)

Marianne Moore: The Poet's Advance (1978)

The Elected Circle: Studies in the Art of Prose (1973)

Yushin's Log and Other Poems (1969)

(edited with introduction)
H.D. Thoreau: A Writer's Journal (1960)

The Design of Democracy (1949)

Justice and World Society (1944)

Collected Poems

Laurence Stapleton

Collected Poems

Riverstone
A Press for Poetry

Grateful acknowledgment is made to the following journals, in which some of these poems first appeared: *The Bryn Mawr Alumnae Bulletin, The Bryn Mawr-Haverford Review, The Honest Ulsterman, The Massachusetts Review,* and *Quixote.*

Edited by Margaret Holley

Published by
Riverstone, A Press for Poetry
1184A MacPherson Drive
West Chester, PA 19380-3814

Publisher's Cataloging-in-Publication
(Provided by Quality Books, Inc.)

Stapleton, Laurence.
    Collected Poems / Laurence Stapleton. -- 1st ed.
    p. cm.
    LCCN: 99-74818
    ISBN: 1-890044-09-1

    I. Title

PS3569.T335C65 1999   811'.54
        QBI99-1102

Printed and bound in the U.S.A. by Bookmasters, Inc.

Over the harbour, found with moment,
A form is far inclined
Speaking some mystery and music
Apparent to the mind.

"The Untaught Teaching"

Contents

Parallel Times and Partial Portraits

Earlier Poems

Ventures Toward America

Parallel Times

and Partial Portraits

A Partial Portrait

As my brother socked him hard,
then tried to wrestle our new neighbor,
Leo, to the ground of the churchyard,
Mrs. Angelli came out with a knife,
and I heard my mother calling softly
from the front door, "Children, children,
come home! Come home!"
"Leo hit him first," I cried.
"Children! Two wrongs don't make a right."
Angellis retreated. We played safe.
Mother descended to the front gate.
She liked proverbs, but not too often.

I thought that she invented them,
or some. Putting on your underwear
inside out just means good luck.
But it's not bad luck to break
a mirror; that superstition
just made you notice disappointments
you wouldn't mind on other days.
And there were better ways to proceed
than walking under a ladder, yet
it's not bad luck; just watch out
for the paint. And no revision
of the song, but it's still wrong
to pray to the saints. But when
the car skidded down the ice-clad
road in circles, and "Jesus Christ!"
he shouted, she said "Your
father isn't swearing, he's really
praying." And she laughed, and then
we did, past fearing.

The Hut

You could park the car
just off the shoulder of the road,
unload a picnic lunch
and start in, tentatively
down the avenue of branches
willing to let a hunch decide
whether to climb up fast
or just walk to the brook
and stay there to eat.
But first look for the turn
to the left, leave the trodden
path as he led us to
the mouldering, half-hewn
timbers, the legendary
hermit's hut. When my father
was sorely visited by some
household wrath, he put on
his hat and coat, calling
from the front door, "If
you behave like that, I'll
spend the night on
the mountain." In the hermit's
hut was not what he meant
but looking at it today
I remembered him singing.
"Where the beavers paddle
on walking canes on the mountain,
way out on the mountain."
We didn't expect him to go,
and he never did – it was just
a grave possibility. "Kiss

4

Susie Jane goodbye
at the fountain, way out on
the mountain." Farther on
the track not too well trod,
not yet steep, you came
to the shining stand
of paper birches, beside
a ripple of water. The troth
with time called us
to ascend; no thought
of unpacking the picnic here.
Nearing an upper rocky
ledge, we spied
a rusty looking stranger
who carried a stick
more purposeful than
the ones we had cut:
The Snake Man. We had
been told of him. Dragging
a heavy canvas sack
he stopped and spoke,
bragging, "I've got plenty
this time" (the rattlers
he collected for pay).
We did not ask to see them
but went on our way
hugging the thermos
as it began to get rainy.
And my father began to sing again,
"I'm going sez I
to that land in the sky
way out on the mountain."

The Parabola

We left our car when the road became impassable.
I for the first time had a chance
to try my snowshoes. Tame, I thought
after the speedy hickory skis. Waddling,
webbing the thick snow with our footsteps,
we two pushed on the sun gilt track without stopping
and by dint of will power reached our goal.
Gazing to right and left we patted the sea
of white to flatten space below the conifers.
There we scattered seed for redpolls, finches,
grosbeaks, crossbills in the punishing weather.
He listened absently to a thin sound,
"Pine siskins." When I told him
I was tired, "Try," he said, "to slide
one foot over the other, more pigeon-toed."
Finally we threw as much as we could on the ground
of the empty pleasure palace, resort of snacks,
and pin-ball games. We both had been consumers
in the flowering season. Now one could taste
and smell the stunned snow, as together
we turned back. We had done what we came to do.

Earlier in the year, in late fall
a diverging stroll left landmarks
behind. We disembarked from the trolley
and left the park on a search for the unexplained
(to me) "wild pigs." The unforbidden
questions I never had the nerve to ask
remained, as we curved away from the mountain
into shaggy undergrowth to find them.
And before long you could see, almost hidden,
the brown shapes grunting, the shiny bristles,

porcine snouts with guttural exclamations.
Were they threatening or beseeching?
I think I wanted it to be a mystery,
not to ask where was a swineherd.
As they rushed forward we stood for a moment
in the anarchy of time, before departing.
The found track now wound down
to an equally deserted orchard. He plucked
an apple. "Taste one – these are wild apples."
Where could I find one again? Tart, unblended,
predicting Northern Spies. Afterwards we trended
away from the range of the mountain, following
a welcome slope that led to the familiar road,
post after post dappled in daylight
changed by the cargo of our foraging.

Time and the Dinosaurs

"It was before your time,"
they said, and the dusty phrase
jarred on my ear. Time
a thing possessed? Abruptly
there flashed before my eye
the footprints planted
in the sandstone shale
between the modern road
and the train tracks, on the
downward slanting ledge,
too hard now to take
the mark of my dirty sneakers.
The thick-clad reptiles
stalked on obsolete legs
balancing with their tails,
some stepping out
with an eight-foot stride.
Sound, unknown. I look
at the hardened witness rock
and at silver pockets of light
in the swirling skirts of the river
– our own Connecticut –
that superseded
their residential swamps.
After the frolic here
in the Triassic mud
leaving these distinct
three-toed memorials
did a meteorite
or a climatic jump
declare them extinct

before the river ever
froze in winter?
People will say
"That was before your
time." A puzzling statement.
Once I was born, I
was never not there.

Nature and Employment

I'm glad to see him
back again - a decent fellow -
and at last he's got a job,
maneuvering the rackety
leaf-blower, or parking it
untended, to roar
its power tool profanity
at fall. Bitted
again, by the follower,
it bobs under trees, scaring
beech and maple offspring
into a mocking pile,
and the children are in school.

A truck arrives
with a suction sleeve.
Clank. Six men shamble
to vacuum the leaves on the bank
into the pickup. But the boss
can't back the thing askew
to inhale red, delete
the partial green,
undo the gold.
"C'mon back!" the groundsmen
steer him, but it sounds like
"Moan. Come, moan." "Back,
back the other way," they bellow
in ethnic tongues, waving
at the headless dragon, told
to eat the suntanned

ransom. The oldest two hustle up
to conjure it and fool
the puzzled young.

Will there be
statues of computers?
monuments to cleaners blowing
instead of the rustling leaves in Erewhon?
Ourselves and one man raking
the weathered fragrance
kids used to jump into and roll over,
our solar valedictory
well-tempered, softly spoken
from a bed of glory.

The Locksmith

Frank Sackcliffe with his tobacco-coloured face
lurked in his dark cubbyhole, taciturn,
the key blanks dangling;
hidden away his many ruses
for opening doors. "Look out, Frank!"
my father called, "That's a tarantula
on your wall – came out of that
bunch of bananas you bought. See?"
Frank blanched, shuddered,
and swept something invisible
from the wall, making the rank
of key blanks jangle. Yet
it was nothing at all but
one of my father's jokes.
I slipped away from Frank's
cubbyhole, laughing at the trick
defused, the scenario
continued. Locked out,
I walked downstairs to the bank,
their landlord, and the store below,
whence the bananas, and the ritual tarantula.

Standard Time

Yes, it happened
on the way to the sunset.
A funny thing – he jumped right
in front of my car – my still quick
reflexes hit the brakes
a paper-thin second before
a tall black skin.

"I ain't homesick yet!"
he laughed his thanks
back on the curb.

Was he black? Am I
the white, bemused
recorder? Sky
darkens early to
a husky red. I steal his words

and drive away. How many
days ahead until
the winter solstice brings
the utmost night?
that must emancipate
next morning, a growing
verb of light, always
myriad-minded, multicolored.

The New Nativity

The crooked arms of the tree
embrace the sky,
and I dare to ponder
how the ungainly
are given grace. My lookout
is just an ordinary room
from which the space above
discloses
sun fire into dimensions
timed by
recurrent love. Waking to
the ever present tense we
live in, I hear
contingent
notes of peace. Resurgent
voices.

Daylight Saving

We're moving toward it, but
where can you bank it?
There is no treasure
except for spending.

Work! while the day is fair.
Shine for the logos.
Mood shall be the more
as our might lessens,
I declare.

I write in January, named for
the two-faced, two-
timing god, and though
the light lengthens, we stay
still, or seem to, in accord
with (see Webster) that mean
solar standard. Ahead
impends the paradox
of the equinox, pretending
a calendar can measure
the unending.

That's for the birds.
We cannot store
the promised extra hour.
It has a right
to come or go
untended.

The skaters reflect the pond

they skate on. Snow intervenes
between us and the light.
O light-preserving snow!

The Summer Owl

I was reading Yeats's prose where he
hides and crosses his own track.
I stared at a large printed page
to raise from names the living men
when, in the second before noon,
I heard an owl, her cracked oboe
inquiry sliding down the scale.
Before I reached the hemlock tree,
she caged her worn lament and flew
soundlessly past, spurning that too
articulate summer light. Then
Yeats and his company returned.

The Black Cherry

Taller than
        the gray monotone
college library
        that stands behind it
our black cherry
        holds deep white
petals on a shield
        of beehive shape
as wide as high
        never weeping
like the red ones
        nor yielding space
to Japanese
        imports. Local
grace a native
        trope
courts every
        printed leaf
opening life
        to mind.

Appearances

Some think those secular
male cardinals have all
the looks. Even bird books
barely illustrate
what coming out females wear.

He flies prime colours to redress
and sublimate snow, or smog,
writes in the decalogue
why Russian speakers say

red means the same
as beauty means, nothing,
seemingly, in between.
He punctuates his word
in black. She is heard

less frequently, but when seen
in daybreak brown and coronet,
she signals that without the queen
no starting gun will fire.
In my great-grandfather's day

the cardinal's northern see,
roughly, was Central Park
New York – but liking new
appearances, they colonized
the mountains, then surprised

the seashore, defying blues
and whistling to dispel the fog.

Red black with orange beak
his yachting colours, fawn brown
her wash and wear. Last week

a friend in Maine told me
the two of them had dropped down
recently, to prospect for
nesting sites at Northeast Harbor.
Conquerors still of the obscure!

Valley Forge in the Bicentennial

The buff-breasted bus-boy from the Sheraton Hotel
— that awkward octagon above the park —
shuffles down the road in tricorne hat,
fingering his flintlock. Forlorn, I miss
the rougher contours of the earlier
land. Leaf-moulded trenches now
retreat in shadow. Signs criss-cross
the old simplistic ways, before
the voyeurism of tall towers
beset Route 23. Cold
log-hut reproductions sacrifice
memory to the hum of tapes. Yet
George Washington at his ark of
decision (absent Lord Howe),
thought first-hand here, and his men
endured the lack of heat, in order
to fire on time; for the bold
inscrutable rapture when
(however little we and TV recapture)
a commonwealth was born.

A Free Ride Home

If I were an admiral I would want to win
in battle. If I'd ever been
a general, I'd feel the same.
Supposing I had the guts to be
a soldier, the flight
deck step to be a sailor, or the wings
to tear the air apart – no question, if
we got engaged, I'd want to win.

But where do you mislocate
a battle – do the strategy people
or the tacticals decide?
or the pearls of intelligence?
I thought I heard Buddy Bolden say
"Open that window
and let the foul air out."

But no illusion.

Spars where the gymnasts outperform,
apartments where the heart is bugged,
can't conceal us from our own conviction.
They are plastic snakes
walking down the road like people.
We have read of the birch trees,
a young girl leaning out of a window.
The code that knocked them back
did not stifle every voice.

Names we need not name to honor.

In the agony of our misapprehension
I recollect or observe
a rain-rutted
brown-road respect for
the right of way, an open space
to turn around. In the clearing
of our faceless fire, we leave
behind no man we sent without us.
We must walk back all the way
to ourselves. We do not abdicate
from freedom. The stork
landing on the roof lightly.

Memory's Ear

I woke up. The air was snoring.
Flying too low again over the
unborn morning
descending to or from where?
Wait and see
the sunstrewn runway; hear
the new sound
daring to land.

The Volunteer's Blues

Blue footprints in the thick white
cumulus overhead let through
a blink of sun. Otherwise
you only see unstinted gloom.
Once upon a time, campaigning
in the smoky autumn weather,
you walked up to a door and rang
the bell. Someone always answered.
You spoke for the cause; they talked
together, pro or con. Tell
me how the so-called culture could
undo what ought to be a country?
Like knowing if you tried to
campaign on that street today,
no one would answer innocently.
You might get shot, turning away
from where they crouch over the big
TV, watching the polls zig-zag,
listening to the only light
they have, the bought sound-bite.

My Great Uncle

Would I recognize him
on a street today?
Probably not.

Out of the door
of a stone building
he would appear,

slight of stature,
sapphire, his
oval eyes.

Surprised, abstracted,
but welcoming un-
heralded callers.

Because, by mistake
I believed him
a blacksmith, by

trade, I looked
for horses stamping,
iron ablaze.

But the few times
I watched the way
up the western

hills were Sundays
when it would amaze
a horse to be shod.

And he never did
make horseshoes.
Instead, he fashioned

bits, bridles,
saddles, head-
stalls, a true

harness-maker
with a racing
clientele. Always

my hope was
to talk with him
apart. My younger

grandfather, this
man's brother, had
served in another

regiment, in the War
between the States,
our common past.

Ransacking the hall
closet, I'd find
the heavy sword.

Once I queried
unfairly, but not
absurdly, I trust,

"Did you ever
kill a Southerner,
Grandpa?" (A calvary

officer, stationed
near Washington.)
He paused. "Child,

pay no mind
to fighting."
Great Uncle Richard,

though, living
far from us,
could have a story

told about him.
And the fact was
he'd been captured

at Cold Harbor,
or was it the battle
of the Wilderness?

I can't recall; he
fought in both.
Half-conscious, near

Andersonville
he heard one
cry, "There's

a Chicopee boy!"
who carried his townsman
into the prison,

giving him water,
sharing what else
he had. In our house,

Grant and Lee,
Jeb Stuart, par
excellence A.P.

Hill, Jackson,
Sheridan, Meade
and Pickett's

brigade stood
side by side
in their books or

stories, on the black
shelves below
the red-clad

upper walls
of my father's study;
the heedless daring

of the South stirring
our hearts
by the leaping

light of the fire,
evenings, to rival
forever the stubborn

valor of the North.
But we were sworn to
the cause of the Union.

Driving our car
up the Berkshire trail
to mend the rarity

of meeting, we hailed
the frail figure
of our great uncle,

a silent man. The
gray building. His
stone-blue eyes.

My Great Aunt

There was the inherited rhyme
she solemnly taught us, yet
of course we could not possibly
know what it meant. She

with her younger brother, John,
sailed to America, luckily,
just before the famine
when she was four, and he

"but two." Her memory
ranged back to the farm
near Cashel, telling
how the Newcomer rode

over the acres lost
in Cromwell's time. Margaret
sitting on the pasture fence,
watched the usurper. But

her words were legendary
rather than bitter. When
first I knew her, she
was old and skittery

but swift of sense, and
would laugh in advance
as we played unintentionally
unkind tricks. For

she was almost blind,
and we loved to rush up
behind her, and untie
the stiff, meticulous apron,

letting her grope for the strings
in a diminutive dance.
As we circled around,
she thanked us for coming

and sang each name.
I was more at ease
with Margaret than any other
in that house, except

my grandfather. It never
occurred to me to wonder
why she wore the apron
and was usually in the kitchen.

Sundays she sat on the right
of Grandmother (the sister-
in-law). I tasted
things to eat we seldom

had at home. While I
drank in the smell of their coffee
mocha and java, grandfather,
in his slow voice, asked

Margaret first, about seconds.
"May I give you
some chicken, Margaret?
Some onions, and parsnips?"

With a sidewise glance
she more than once replied,
"If you can spare it, John."
I suddenly understood

her knee-high vision
from the rail, while Baron
what's his name cantered
across their land.

To the last she would relate
the legends so real
to her, and project their
future ends. "Yet

never forget," she'd say,
"you're . . . ." But I won't spell
that famous infamous name.
When I was able to read

whatever I liked, Margaret
had been gone for years.
Absorbed by the fate
of Tess of the D'Urbervilles,

I guessed what Thomas Hardy
was thinking of. No fear,
Aunt Margaret wouldn't
have had to concede

to nature's unheeding
mistake. With no claim
or desperate need, because
she could spare it for us

collateral children, she founded
an ancestry of love.

Under Quabbin

Lying diagonally
> against the ale brown
upright boards
> of the abandoned
dam once he
> leaned too far
fell
> into the stream
I hoarding
> the mobile sounds
reel clicking on
> the rod's wrist
of the big man who
> suddenly dropped it
to lift his child
> out of the no longer wild
river. The Sunday
> Boston Globe stood
weighted beneath the maple
> where her quiet glory
sat reading the recipes
> before the valley flooding
for that city to drink
> and our site near Pelham buried
begetting only
> this dream of the hollow
her startled head followed
> my father as he steered
their dripping son toward
> the red farmhouse hearth

I did not hurry
                up that now drowned hill
looking from earth below to
                skylight I admired
him because he said "Pelham"
                it was his birthday rite to choose
I didn't think he
                had it in him he was four
his hair shone like more
                than just a brother
until today's vast reservoir
                told the eagle to return
immortally whistling
                the plot of a positron
running
                backward in time
to go
                asymmetrically forward.

Cézanne: Retrospectively Forward

The sun flew down the skylight on its own diagonal.
The sea before L'Estaque deepened its blue.
On some canvasses white clouds grew
Brighter, waving heights of illumination.
Not far, a shadowy green line announces

The summit of Cézanne's mountain, Sainte-Victoire,
Revealing the intensity he said unfolded
To him. One painting with pointed arches
Of trees, or a curve of coast, called for others
To prove it living forever in a different guise.

In Valabrègue's portrait or his own,
An inescapable identity looks
From the pitch-black pupils of their eyes;
And Madame Cézanne in a garden wore
Sadness and honor in a striped dress.

Cézanne observed motifs of cubes and spheres
In the silent whereabouts of roads and houses.
But he did not try to work on cloudy days;
He said they hindered his research. Indoors
The cup of life spilled from pears and apples,

Obstreperous table cloths, wine bottles.
In later years his watercolors built
Upswinging boulders with strokes racing
Downward, in beautiful stormy conjunctions of form
That still brave out the time-space.

In the Paper City
For Charles and Brenda Tomlinson

When the Boston capitalists dammed the river,
it breathed deeply behind the barrier,
and before you could look, the dam gave way.
Next time they made it with a concrete
foot, heavier timber, sheets
of boiler plate over the top.
Now when gates closed, the water
complied, hissing over the dam,
after first obeying orders
to fill two levels of canals.
Factories soaked up the power
and walled in a company town
unaware of itself. "Boarding houses"
for the "help" rose out of the ground; girls
left country farms to earn their keep.
Agents abroad booked spinners
for skilled hands to make cloth,
and found papermakers, too, for the jobs,
plentiful except in bad times
when scores and scores of English, Irish,
Polish, and French arrivals from Canada
were laid off. In better times
children rubbed sleepy eyes
sent to labor in the mills from dawn
to sunset, poor tykes
– the hunger strikes to win a ten-hour
hour day beyond their grasp.

Rowena Ravine lived on the avenue,
Main Street, that cut through
the mill district. Tall, impassive,

her face seemed waiting to be lighted
by some unforeseen event. I never
visited her down there;
yet I liked her; she
felt the hiatus between us more
than I. We had nothing in common
but our Girl Scout uniforms and marching
behind the flag on the Fourth of July.
Main Street people with their many
bilingual kids were not meant
to be entertained by any show
of civic glory. But Rowena's friends
saw the skidrow red-nosed clowns,
the spangled ladies linking hands
across cavorting horses, the elephants'
soft-shoe shuffle, and heard
the jangled tune of the steam calliope
before we did, and ran for a chance
to watch again in the upper city.
I was stunned when a classmate told me
Rowena's father had tried to murder
her mother with a butcher's knife.
They had wanted everything for Rowena
and left her this ragdoll
heart. I think he was a tailor
working alone, not in the mills.
The blue-eyed mills! Their flumes
disgorging sulphate and sulphite
spat at the dark canals: that once
living water now sewn up
in brick, far from its start
seaward from the Connecticut Lakes,

flowing through all the invading
chemicals made to give
more capital to the capitalists
and pay to the undaunted poor.

In the twilight of good years the men
crowded through the gate in overalls
and long-sleeved shirts. When
you walked or drove past, the sultry
air hummed and vibrated with
the sound of bobbins turning, spindles
reaching, rollers revolving. In the morning
the deep-toned hollow whistle
rousing the day shift haunted
my waking ear. On my way to school
to skirt the square block sheltering
Wisteriahurst, anemic mansion
of Belle Skinner, instilled a silent
teaching. She collected violins.
Skinner's satins already draped
thousands of women. Farr Alpaca
lined prosperous coats. Crocker
McEllwain's stony embrace
held a proud classmate's
mother, who earned her bread. The mills!

The blue-eyed mills! The indigo panes
and cloudy canals. By free choice
I felt an exile in the city.
The valley and surrounding hills
housed my spirit, but I had been
partly baptized by the winding canals,

innoculated by the mule spinners,
crowned hit or miss by the papermaking
wasps of Whiting's Eagle A bond.
I still buy expensive paper
even for rough drafts like this.

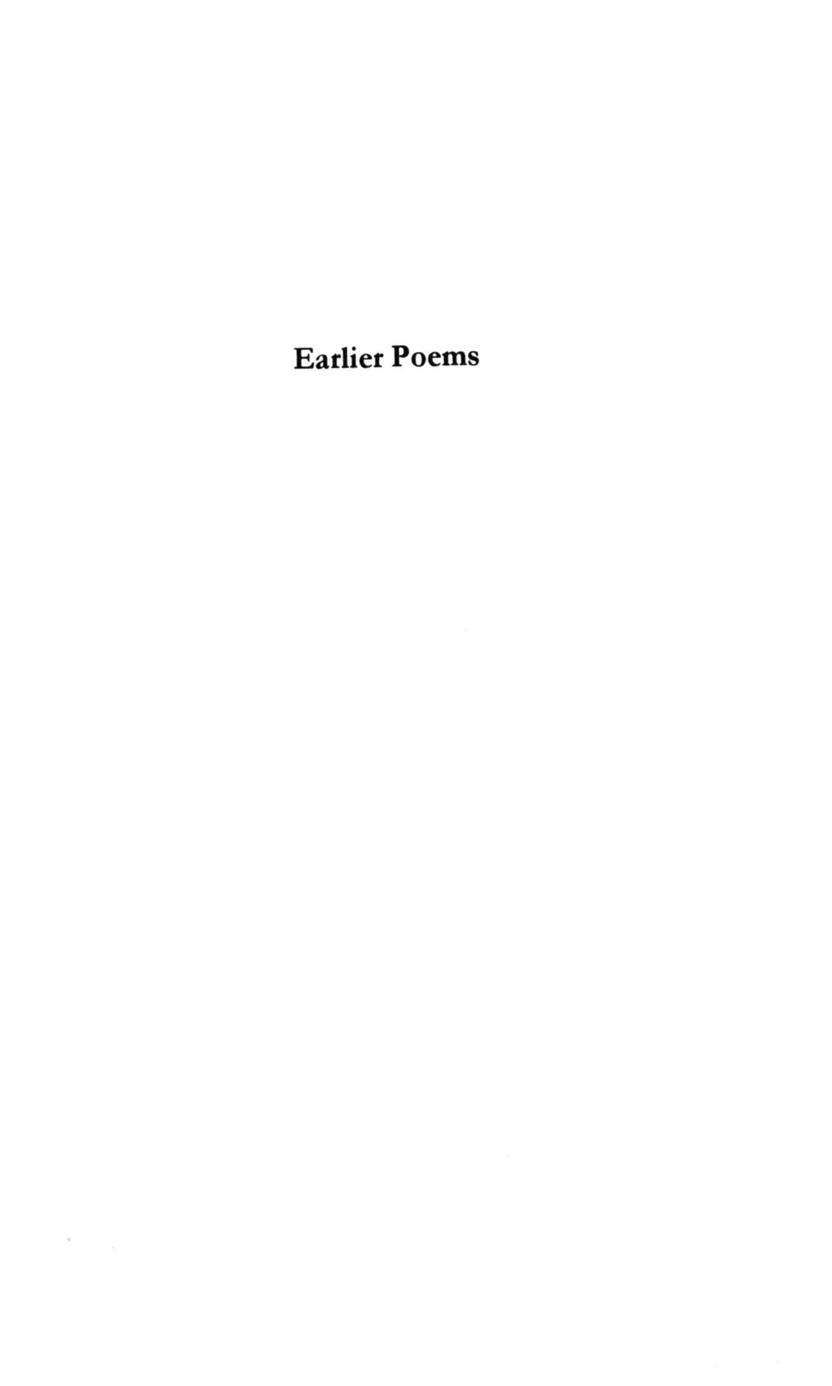

Earlier Poems

Along the Coast

The cloud-caught pools, the rosy island and pale moon,
The flowing bay in evening fantasy
Leaving the promontory for the open tide
Propose an old, untamed elation.

This sail, this harrow of geese that down the harbour
Flexing the wind intend it visible,
Follow my thought into a forward form
And shake direction on the unknown water.

Like cloth, rough firmness soothingly
Shelters the deep, roofing the dense marine
To walk upon for angels, but for landsmen
A miracle because it's only seen.

Shoreward upon the sand to stand
Or climb the steep path is liberal;
Sky plants its image in the dark lagoon,
Osprey and air speed down. We mark

A greener wave reminds the sea-toned bell:
Night's landfall spins the moment of "All's well."

'The Eagle Must Have an Educated Eye'

Rim-rounding from cloud
In a slow power-float, he
Suddenly stepped up to high, his
Impossible try trumpeting to a
Crescendo and a close
Over some somber, leaf-grown
Sun-pale sweep of time
In a November earth-space.

Men call that fact.

As the flat-winged white head
Bright tail dives for the duck
And the duck submarines the lake,
That is the arc of moment to take
Lightly – for to see is to see first,
The far-trained eagle said,
Not to explain.

For Marion Edwards Park

(With a gift of music from several of her friends)

Slowly
Field these seeds of light and sow upon the water
Invisible influence, magical, musical.

And mark
Moon islands in the sky of time where night
Arches the bay with silence, rhythmical.

And sound
Within the wooded grain the heavenly ember
shapely in the fire of listening, lyrical.

Amaze
With joyful harmony those who gather in this house
And distant friends in union, mystical.

And join
In union with the rarest star of peace
Man and the Maker, indivisible.

The Crazy Daisies

The crazy daisies
improve again
their cavorting on
the wide champaign.

A leaf-sprung, sprinting
thoroughfare
cantilevers
winds to air.

Rivers margin
the far meander;
amber drift of
light or sand or

inwrought blossoms'
thoughtful edge
elbow the sea-bent
river's ledge.

A compass, in
the sun's degrees,
cuts paths between
land-locked trees

and we discover
how to praise
sun the rhymer's
rhyming ways

which crazy daisies
prove again
swaying on the
wide champaign.

Marsden Hartley and Howard Gray

New Englanders move, sometimes go west
Or sometimes south, but up in the hills
Along the valleys, beside the fields,
Or in cities straddled across the rivers
Enough remain, as fiery still
The ancient crucible burns for America
Forging no longer the Puritan armour
But a spiritual strength that makes for form.
Reserve in people is not always coldness.
It can be warmth told with simplicity,
Lasting invincible heart, tough
Humour, resilience, and the power to believe.

At sixty-five, a retired professor
New York State bred, and trained at Harvard,
Historian charged with modern anxiety,
"My name is Howard," you said politely
As we walked to the movies, thereby
Becoming more dignified. Hard to describe
Any man one has known, hardest a shy
Conscience like yours; disciplined habit;
Exact eye and brow of worry;
Turning the vase in the light
You knew how the clay was fired.

In the last months, Howard, you were often remembering.
You told me you studied with William James.
We sat on the porch one lowering August evening
Under the Pennsylvania trees, during the war.
Your Marsden Hartley on my wall
Brings the richness and motion of all New England.

Red-tufted trees of Maine in autumn
Climb the dark slope of the mountain
To purple islands of clouds convening
In awe of existence. Salute it!
Past or present, the silent dynamo.

Visit to a Quaker Meeting

Just look at that
Cardinal practicing up in winter.
Most red or beautiful of birds
In this still grey, that rich whistle stopping
Short of the last full exclamation, he breathes
Triumphant downbeat in spring; yet anything
So warm as this preparatory note in January dazzles
Our thirst, is first, is cardinal
In form and colour. How like the kept fire
Ready even in this cold, is joy, is art, and you say
"Just look at that! Isn't that wonderful!"

Inside the meeting house the grey
Gathers into a visible silence, a weighty
Whirlpool of attention, a wondering
For the willing stranger among the Friends.
Her still mind fluctuates between her peace
                              and their possession,
Unpracticed in their ways and pondering
Respectfully, whether in their wholly admirable
Waiting, any revelation, light, fire, love is born.
Expectedly it seems an elder and an upright man
Speaks of the psalms; the word Selah he says
Is hard to translate but important; it means
In Hebrew "Just look at that! Isn't that
Wonderful!" Clearly he knows many books,
Is moved as a good scholar a good man is moved.
Eighty years old he says religion makes a stronger body.

Further into the silence that closes around the speaking,
The newcomer wishes a window in the wall, a through light

Joining the inner light. To celebrate
Selah, the fullness of the world
Searches one with more power. This charity
With which all calmly hear the hysteric lady
Who interrupts us next, exclaiming
"Arise, make a song, like Deborah!"
This charity is a modern sensible compassion.
There is a deeper that ennobles and amazes us,
This mad lady's forebears had it, when they quaked
                    and trembled.

Liking the absence of mummery, preferring
The simple sword of truth to the encrusted scabbard,
The stranger is yet away from the one
Word, accent, sound or song or cardinal –
The reverential greeting. It is not here
Though stronger because there are some here. At the end
Shake hands with these friends and harbour the trust of feeling
In that larger meeting. Selah!

On Certain Modern Writers and Philosophers

Pity the man who makes God the compensation
For all that he fears and hates in life,
Twisting a knife in each bright sensation,
Scolding any song because his own soul is in strife,
Despising with determined afterthought
Dance light he knows not.

(Calvin was mild compared with Freud.)
Emancipated by science, he worries about his dreams
Neglecting new deeds, to annul and to avoid
The stronger need that led to pastures of contentment.
The heart that could digest both action and fulfillment
He replaces by the art of gilding what seems.

But the command is to forgive the snared magician
Who is scheming and dreaming, unaware of his toil.
Though in the concrete he curses love and every victory,
Help him if we can to be undeceived
And with the steadfast effort of plainfelt sense
Dissolve his unrequited, his voluptuous penitence.

For if faith is the evidence of things unseen
There is more to obey in the possible connections
That link what we spring from, the earth and its enchantment
With the goodness of true men, both those we know
                  and strangers,
And their unexpected bravery, that fights with death
                  and sadness.
It comes as a gift and raises us to gladness
Where they stand on the revetment and do not regret
                  their birth.

Of conjoined energies leading up to man
God (if deity be nameable)
Who is the word, the origin of author,
Says to the prophet practicing his trade,
There was joy in the morning when the stars sang together
And many times I have renewed the lapsing world.
Why will you despair? And wither in the shade?
I cannot leave all this that love began.

The Untaught Teaching

"The operations of Heaven are profoundly mysterious. . . .
it has water levels for levelling, but it does not use them; it has
plumblines for setting things upright, but it does not use them
. . . . it works in deep stillness. Thus it is said, Heaven has no
form and yet the myriad things are brought to perfection. This
may be called the untaught teaching."[1]

Some people love abstraction who have nothing
                     to abstract from.
To them a spire of wire or a twisted eggshell is pure;
They find resemblance and recognition obscure,
Prefer to bleach the city bones and pull them apart.
Broad hoops of bridges demand to be set down
In a wilderness bare of people, or a town
Of absentees, where an old man bent like a cart
Is no model to pose for the role of a clown.

Subdue your wit, some say, to the magnetic mart
Exercising its irrelevant selection
Of the bones nerves sinews most likely to succeed.
Remember that a smart capitalist makes an excellent
                     art collector.
He approves abstraction with its planes of zoned attraction;
Wondrously beside the striped sea it paints
On the deserted beach an orange rind as if it had been woven.
– Decoration may be daring if feeling is restrained.

ii

Is nothing spoken under the fawn gray hasp of stone
Arching the pent river, and the marshalled brick
Of planned apartments pinioned in lone
Red rectangles on the risen shore?
And I heard the visiting philosopher remark, "When we say
There is a man over there in the distance, we really mean
There is a finite probability that he is a man.
But if you take the example of a distant pigeon – "
His voice and manner were modest, his eyebrow soared.
In the marshes, reflecting into the rivulet, Stygian,
A notable hummock crowned by a billboard
Proclaims to the weary traveller its solicitude
In pastel neon, lest he suffer a cold.
Beckoning in the forest of pylons and telegraph poles,
Earthly transmission, aerial dilemma,
Definite above the chemical fog of Newark
The startling rib of highway brings many home.

iii

Curious thus how sentimental the city and its approaches
Where the leaning sunlight lays its gentle touch
On the vaunted buildings, and much of the day
Is given its due in the corner store or the newsstand
Sheltering the passerby as a tent a warrior.
The streets wearing their smoky nostalgic plumes
Lead off the slipping mist to the river, where the sun

Making a last play and stubborn show of sunset, said,
'There are fellows who know how to be decent here'
Where the great assembly on the sea debouches.

iv

Over the harbour, found with moment,
A form is far inclined
Speaking some mystery and music
Apparent to the mind. And without torment
Or emptiness, man sees to invest the space
With likeness of his strength and his intention.
Traversing sea and air, throughout the firmament
Time quickens into impulse and to act
In every finite instant of creation.
The untaught teaching nourished an orphan – the abstract.

[1] Lu Shih Chhun Shhiu, Trans. Joseph Needham.

Relating to Plymouth

I

A cloud that was made by nature, not by man,
Must have emerged from the endearing vagueness,
Sky, and longer than I am likely
To sit watching, it will probably
Appear, and disappear, in innumerable
Small new guises over that strip of sand
That separates bay from sea.
A sandbar – yes – interrupting the uninterrupted
Vista by which we might think we could look
Almost to Europe, and be more satisfied
We would suppose, with this blink of it all
In one, and be mightily deceived.
Sandbar with its temporary-seeming, not too
Symmetrical houses that a painter would decide
To put in, if they weren't there,
To show that sandbar as good as it really is,
Standing where Champlain mapped it. Ocean-engineering.

II

Its economical green and sandmixed ochre,
No sophistication of chrome, but veritable terreverte,
Stretch on a diagonal parallel to the other
Outer-gray, heather gray, island humped
Diagonal ending in the Gurnet. This
Charted identity, seeable shore, is part of why
Pilgrims we tire of hearing about and can't imagine

Landed and stayed, although Felicia Hemans
                    (an Englishwoman)
Wept, when she heard the coast was not rock-bound.

III

A drop – there might be a neutron in it –
I don't know, some configuration of thicker
Damp than the background sky, and yet thinner
Than the evenly-bevelled water that's
Steadying the tide – a few of these samples
Of something are furrowing the upperside
Of that cloud, tending a curve or two
Of white more solid than the underside where
That look of disappearing again might
Fool you, if you don't see the pigment touched in there.
Gray? Firmer than gray, confirming
As the wind ruffles the sea shapes
That mostly everything is blue here
Except sails, hulls, houses cut into the blue
And the pines, the grass, the bayberries surrounding it.
But the blue of the sea, the sea invented for itself.

IV

If the cloud made by nature not by man
Leads on a company of clouds, no particular
Man-made metaphor seems to do
But won't be needed. There's rhythm,
And inattention is permitted. Sounds
Of a well-tuned transport move companionably

With the ancient steamboat's motor.
A gull inaudibly walking with cautious feet, as if
To avoid the mud, the sky-brown tide-flat, enhances
the light-flake elegance of terns, dipping along the track
Of invisible minnows. White is motion here
Not sound, but sound is change
Like the keys of the wind's voice. Now
The cloud dabs pink high over the sandbar
And turns a three-quarter turn seaward.
And later it will be, if red,
Nothing that carmine is a word for.

A cloud made by nature doesn't say much.
"Something will come again." That's all.

The Open Blue Collar
1933, 1993

Late afternoon. I see
the warmth pass from the face of the stone,
while the light remains. A bird on a branch above
is chipping and shaping a sound like a rubbed seed
away from the tide of voices spread from the factory door
and the city stir.

People are strung from the door like a breaking wave,
walking away from the mill, a day's work over.
And where is to be seen
the body of moon for this tide?

In the spring, in the year's high season
yet once again
the dead awaken
and speak, and summon time
when more than sun the light itself revealed
the sinewy skills of old and young
fastened in beam and girder, stone and tower.
Was this their story?

Or say that heavy with intent the angel
unrolls the stone and unbuilds the tower.
More mysterious than any prophecy
what beam, strained into its unstrained hold,
what pile and mortar and weight record:
before love, before knowledge is labor.

Look back; and passing the mountains
a rider dismounts at the good end of news

or falls with the feather: is the battle decisive?
The people resolve and march to the sea
fulfilling the legend of travel, although no cause
takes heart in the saga.

Yet from press or kiln, idle hoist or plow,
foundry or factory, mine or quarry,
the tides surge higher now
of the hunger for work, on the sand of history.

Men and American Egrets Fishing

Hours curve into a tawny embrace;
Anglers inch along the shore, test lines
In the swung hollow where the creek,
Crumb Creek, smooths out to
A reservoir, back of the dam. Signs
Define a restricted area; thus far
O.K. with the water company's guards,
Whose traffic-cop whistles turn skeptical heads.
We trespass, diviners
Of the natural right, a fisherman's walk.

Alert egrets explore the pond unconcerned.
If casters compete, they volplane with slow
Finesse, trailing black landing gear.
Hours unclasp, race.

"My minnie's not working."
An elder of the weekend fraternity
Groans in the heat. He
"Calls her in for inspection."
The young man watches him winding, winding,
A home-made reel. "Pappy, have some good."
He offers a twist of tobacco, and the elder
Smells it, and notes with surprise,
"I like this kind. How much does it cost
At the cut-rate?

Well no wonder
I pay that much for a pound can."
"Yeah?" says the Georgian, "I can't smoke it
If it's got no flavour."

A papery sleeve
Snakes the line away from him. "Hey, don't
Throw away my bait. If I can't catch nothin'
I'll eat the bait when I git to home."

Sometimes considering from a Chinese
Mount of speculation, or hook-bent
On the shore itself, the gifted egrets
Touring from the South, fix those
Transparent minnows with their spears of gold,
And rise at sundown to compose
An octave in the tree (each year the same)
Below the sheared lamb on the hill farm.

War-Time Pastoral

Within the span of universal weather,
Not only light and warmth and air
But all that sun, moon, stars together
Move to create, the widest to compare
With local being, I call my thoughts to wake,
And since it is spring, and life wills to unfold
To simple fields a wondering question, take
To the green garden and the thickets where
Robins rehearse their summer phrases in the cold.

Rain in the cup of the leaf, the sun a globe
Of antique moment in the solemn dew,
A gazing instant in each pendant lobe
In light, informal motion, bright and new
Bids us to dance with it and lose no time,
The more that days and weeks are unforetold,
Which sets us with our better selves to rhyme
But rise from farther source than any view,
A curious fact, as if nothing had ever grown old.

This restless passion, the love of life, requires
A time to think at large, a place to be
Far from the wasting business, work that hires
The voice, the pen, the judgment, not to see
Beyond itself, but stay in useful bounds,
The staple of the world, and yet we know
Sometimes there must be vacancy that sounds
The swinging of our hearts when they are free
And tunes the willing ear when distant measure blow.

A soldier and his girl walk arm in arm
And even death must whisper, "By and by,"
Their looks and thoughts oblivious of the swarm
Of alien guns on metal wings that fly.
The heavy furrows where the dark command
Takes us to lean against that somber sky
They walk with careless footfall in the spring,
Though suffering is continuous with this land,
These few brief hours for them the best of anything.

For love and grace are serious and return.
This going forth of impulse undefined
As if a deeper pattern to discern
Gives compass to my path, the way to find
Your living word, and seed and ground to sow.
If elsewhere mine-laid miles are Godforsaken
And men teach earth to kill rather than grow,
Hope has a braver music to unwind
Across the upland meadow where the song was spoken.

Orange Is Like Gold, Gold Like Orange

Behind my shoulder, something speaks
alive, like snow.
Imagine, in the float of air
it disappears, while near,

convoyed, although by few.

Old alchemists we seldom read
found in gold a means of change
to make a lease hold
from element to element

on their perfection bent.

Yet orange, in sun's rheostat,
refutes the speed;
something nearer living fire,
home run in sight,

prepares to turn space round.

Gold is curved or squarer than
a circle or a star.
But orange is like breathing through
your eyes, or standing in a wood

crowned, like a warbler.

When trees uphold the colour's fall
in bare, unwoven symmetry,
their angles and high interval
dam a reservoir of light,

raise light to be their repertoire.

The 'Occasional' Chair

An office chair I have seen a thousand days
and more, its hooped and hairpin marl
of faded wood, at last has prised the hour
of sudden splendor, where it stands
happening to be in a novel spot beside
my window. The yellow trends of light
and dark diagonal burl of shadow
find here a chance to ray themselves
incomparably. And the dumb chair, their
conductor, conciliates their ways.

Late Snow Before Easter in the Italian Garden

I

The birds are puzzled as we are
The second day of spring
By snow filtering, lacing the air
With itself, surprising spaces
Tentatively. The delicate traces
Of novelty in old time.
The birds, like maces,
Bob and dare. The chime of a church
Unwanted by us, replaces
Silence we care to keep untold.
The crow benights the white.
A redbird hones its whistle sweet.
A mockingbird flares.

II

I remember vaulting the wall
Beyond the field on the old estate, where
Nuns also bob and stare
In their keep. I steal, pace
To smell the magnolia stellata
Down to an inappropriate final
Circle. There they stand
The unsold pagan statues. Juno assailed
Expecting some egress? Or
Aware of a negative all?
The incredulous day prevailed.

III

The snow retreats, uncovers
Reborn snowdrops: the pale, the purple crocus revives,
Unwary again, unwarned.
The bees return to them. Where have
The bees kept themselves in the snow? Small boys
Shout on bicycles wheeling. Children
Meet in their own convention, while
Teenagers fly to Florida. Downstairs
The quiet baby, he too, prematurely born,
Cries! He is still alive. Cries!
I wonder, I love, I hear
The all going on of it, whole
On the day before Easter.

The First Day in Oregon

My brother was on a ladder hammering
When I suddenly heard the silver chords of the hermit thrush.
My startled ear placed its newborn melody elsewhere at first,
But it is one country, I told myself, for the birds
                              and the beasts.

And who are we?

Ventures Toward America

YUSHIN'S LOG

The lighthouse and three volcanoes bore to the
North and West, when we sailed from Avacha.
Our signals we knew for speaking in
fog, or if met by strange ships.
The council of officers feared the course
set for Company Land, a coast
Juan de Gama believed he had seen
in mid-Pacific. Was it America?
No one could tell where North America
ended, or whether it might be joined
to Russia.

        Before he died, the Emperor
Peter the Great had planned this voyage
to see if the continents were united,
or, if separate, how far apart.
Early in June, our ships kept station.
Vitus Bering, the Captain Commander,
led in his two-masted brig, the *St. Peter;*
Captain Chirikov in the *St. Paul*
steered beside us. Fog, and we beat
the bells and leaned to the low tattoo
of drums, our language, and so directed
the vessels held on the hidden way,
as we drew our track on a map of the world.
The officers all distrusting the route
gazed due East, with a sailor's instinct.
There the natives we knew in Kamchatka

pointed us the way to Nova Zembla,
"new land," but the bookish astronomer,
de la Croyère, prevailed with Peter
who had ordered our captain to bear to the South.
In the third week of June a clamoring gale
misled the ships before midnight.
Clewed up foresail, hove to. Through the morning
we rocked in the wind as it reefed the sky.
Sun sank the bell through the fog, and fasting, it
died. Light made day its invention.
We searched for the consort but looked into nothing,
unable to mark the stir of a ship
in the shifting water. Because of the wind
we could not beat back to the place where we parted;
for days we searched with lookout on topmast.
Then Captain Bering, the patient commander,
asked advice from the council of officers.
Waxel, the Swedish Lieutenant, second
in command, had real control of the ship,
while Bering counted days in his cabin
through sickness; the years of labor in Siberia
preparing for the voyage, had exhausted him.
Then the fleetmaster, Khitrov, and I, the assistant
navigator, Yushin, went below.
With others we signed a paper (it was
the custom, in the Russian Imperial Navy
to protect ourselves and the Commander)
showing that we had decided to steer
South again to the forty-fifth parallel,
where we hoped to confirm the conjured land

Juan de Gama dreamed in this latitude.
But we crossed the unspeaking waves without sign.
The maps proved false, and we privately cursed
the gullible Hamburg cartographer – he
lengthened our track. Sounding, we left
no bottom in ninety fathoms. No drift
of wood or succulent weed encouraged us.
I saw the ducks' formation flying
that afternoon, as the Captain Commander
ordered the course held one more day.
No land rose. Then Bering changed
the compass setting to North and East,
as the officers would have originally spoken
if they could have ignored the foreign Professor
de la Croyère, that conceited astronomer.
He thought the maps he brought from Europe
more to be trusted than sailors' experience.
His lot was not cast with us, but with Chirikov
in the ship that had disappeared in the fog.

Supplies began to give out in July.
Even before we embarked, a mishap
in crossing the Okhotsk River had lost us
our biscuit. Our ships, built in Kamchatka,
had scanty place for stores, which shortened
the practical span of exploration
to this one summer; and Bering had chosen
to return in September to Russian quarters.
Fog, rain, and the stripe of the sun
banded the easterly seaway. A whale

floated dead in the trough of the ship.
Gulls rode the carcass. As our casks of water
lightened, we prayed for a landfall
and rationed the crew. The captain lay
in his bunk, enduring the toil while Waxel,
the Swedish lieutenant, conned the ship.
I do not know who first saw the land.
We spun together and steered for it.
Word was brought to the captain, "A cape
darkens the East!" on Elia's day.
It was part of an island, America's offspring
alone in the sea like a column of stone.
The continent moved still away. But we,
sailing from the West, first encountered
the ramparted range, the cloud-clipped
Mt. St. Elias, nature's snow turret.
We traced on our chart a mark for America
north of any hitherto known
boundaries of that land.

              For Bering,
this was the second of two expeditions
in North Pacific mapless waters.
Near triumph, we saw him shrug his doubt.
Not unaware of achievement, he feared
he could not complete the task that the Emperor,
and after him Catherine the Great, laid upon us.
We reviewed our orders to find a settlement
of Europeans, if any were there.
From them we must learn the name of the coast,

but the Empress told us, "never explain
to the people you meet with the way to Kamchatka."
We thirsted for water. Lowered the long boat
south of the island and hauled the barrels.
Bering turned away from our cheers.
He lacked muscle to foot the soil
of his new discovery. He scoffed at the mention
of gold, or rarer minerals, scanning
not land but the sky and the calendar.
No time, he said, to hunt for natives.
Then the German, Steller, a troublesome scientist,
accosted him, insisting on his right
to study the island. He shouted roughly,
"Your Highness begged me to come on this voyage
and forbade me to go to Japan as I wished
with Captain Spanberg. You swore
you wanted a naturalist, and I would be the first
to examine land in the North Pacific.
Having studied Kamchatka for many years,
I am the one man able to compare
this coast, to win honor for Russia. Are you
afraid? Or, for the second time,
too spirit-spent to pursue the unknown?"
Then the captain waved him on shore
with jokes, and mock salutes, and he threatened
to abandon anyone who delayed
his return and the discipline of the ship.

In wrath, the footloose philosopher then
ran like a hare and climbed and wound,

as he found any clue to collect his specimens.
He travelled unarmed, with a single Kossack,
his servant. When abruptly they stumbled
on underground huts, absolute proof
absolved our aim. For men lived here
but had disappeared. Had they then built
these sandy dugouts for summer quarters?
Steller raked the relics of fire,
he cherished the fragments of reindeer bones,
he sniffed at bits of fish, to question
the fellows who had just moved out. Avid
he collected stone arrows and the tools
they had fashioned for cutting trees and thongs
of fiber. These people did not want art.
He went with these specimens back to the ship.
Then Steller – oh, no doubt, a scholar,
but stubborn and too persistent – reminded
the captain that Peter the Great had ordered
courtesy to the natives, and he insisted
that presents be left in exchange for the trophies.
The captain agreed, and then red silk,
tobacco, and a kettle were hauled to their huts.

Meantime, on a neighboring island, the fleetmaster,
Sofron Khitrov, commanded a party
loading water for the homeward voyage
and discovered tracks of men and a running
fox. He followed, and found subterranean
lodgings, neatly lined in wood.
He brought back a shovel, a basket, a stone.

Their mountains lifting trees aloft
rise higher than the barer Siberian coast.
Some began to say we should winter there.
Adjunct Steller pushed his advice
to unload the stores. Here we had timber
and water, and could hunt and explore at will,
and trade with the people, and be more likely
to survive by waiting it out in America.
But Steller knew nothing of navigation,
or men, or the scope of the expedition
so far prolonged. Ten years we had spent
dragging the poods of flour and precious
supplies across the body of Russia,
and building a fleet, and preparing a depot
at Petropavlovsk. The commander,
old in hardship, reckoned the scanty
stores and observed the homesick men.
He feared that westerly winds would delay
our passage back to Kamchatka. At last
he made up his mind, and we steered for Asia.
His course obeyed the trend of the coast
to the north and west and would secretly trace,
as we were ordered, a chart of its contour.

But again the original map misled us.
We could not make to the north. Monstrous
waves assailed the rocks. At night
calmer waters alarmed us, unwarning
of hazards. We dreaded shallows in fog.
We woke each day to ignorant latitudes.

Waxel, who conned the boat, could seldom
sleep. Sometimes he anchored in darkness.
Once we avoided wreck at midnight
narrowly, standing off a suspected
island, and in the morning we saw it
and named it Toumannoi, foggy one.
Now a sense of suffering came on the crew,
starved, unfit for cruel watches
in the shrouded air. We buried the first,
a seaman, Schumagin, when, lacking water,
we hove back sixty miles to a crumbling
island. At least we made it his monument.
We found brackish stuff near the marshes.
Steller, as usual, argued we should go
inland, where he claimed he had cleared a spring.
But the captain would not delay the ship.
That night, the lookout gazing north
spied a bud of fire. We reckoned
where it grew in the dark. At dawn we
lowered the yawl, our fleetmaster Khitrov
commanding. Constable Roselius, along with
a canoneer, and a Kamchatkan linguist
were his party, and soldiers and sailors.
Bering rose to draft their orders,
and equipped the party for barter: bells,
knives, mirrors, boxes, and tweed.
At this time we had held the sea ninety days.
We had seen no men but ourselves. If now
we came on Americans, we would fulfill
Peter the Great's impossible orders.

Khitrov at first was unsuccessful,
though he traced his path as far as fire
deserted by the people.

                       The empty wind
twisted to the vortex of a gale.
The yawl splintered on the rocks. Our comrade
Russians, ashore, wept when they saw us
get under canvas and swing the ship
and depart from them to seek anchorage. Oddly,
our Chukchi interpreters reassured them,
believing us, their shipmates, honest.
We rescued the lot in the longboat; the damaged
yawl forever remained on that shore.
Perforce we struck our yards in the storm
that night and anchored. A naked cry
bounced from the black rocks.
                             Americans!
In the long-sought morning, all who could walk
crowded to the rail, as two of the strangers
paddled to the ship, sealed from the waves
in canoes of skin, smooth, symmetrical.
They gashed our ears with guttural cries
in a madman's pitch. We took for granted
that our Chukchi speaker would understand them;
indeed, he did have the same creased
nose and fold of eye, and clothing
not unlike, but when he spoke to them
they made signs that their ears were deaf.
Nor would they board the ship, but beckoned

toward land, with promising gesture of food.
The one we believed to be chief bedaubed
his face with paint and fanned with a stick
of red-coloured spruce, polished, topped by
wings of a falcon. Then he lofted it
toward our vessel. We lowered trinkets.
They all held high the falcon's body.
We dropped a mirror into the sea.
Abruptly, they paddled back to the shore.
Bering gave the command to follow.
Our party embarked with arms concealed
under canvas, and biscuits and gin to offer
to the tribe, knitting their dance on the sand.

Reassured by a racket of greeting and signs
of welcome, three of our party waded
to the savage assembly, while the rest of us rode
in our boat, unable to land in the wind.
The islanders pointed to a hill, where their huts
stepped back from the shore in curious rows
designed for defense. They scorned
our gifts and spat out the gin in disgust.
But they offered our fellows a piece of blubber
from the whale; we were hungry and ate it.
All the while the tribe, arrested in wonder,
plucked at the garments of the three on shore.
It was as if the whole body
were an eye, and we were before them acting
in an antique miracle. They devoured our every

casual twist or word. No doubt now
these men were Americans.

                  The screen of evening
unfolded across the rain, and Waxel
summoned us back to the boat. But the islanders
blocked our path with raw unwelcome
pieces of blubber and suggested we smear
our bodies with pigment. We refused,
and they seized the painter of our boat, but whether
to haul us on shore or destroy us
we could not read their intention. Worse,
they seized our interpreter; of course
he looked more like them, than like us,
but he fought to be free and implored us to save him.
We had to move and fired three muskets
in the air; three times the cliffs collected
the report, and the islanders fell as if hit.
We ran to the boat and beat away,
laughing, as we watched them rise unharmed.
At night their fire shattered the rain.
We hauled away in thickening weather,
the savages shouting uncouth farewell.
Now the winds marched out of the West,
as Bering had feared, and the two-masted brig
rocked aslant the ravening waves.
When the watch changed, the crewmen struggled
to stand, weak from hunger. Often
comrades carried the helmsman forward,

and he sat in a chair to steer. The shrouds
frayed in the wind No one had arms
to bend on canvas. We lowered sails
to save the masts and made less headway.
The Captain Commander pitied the crew
and pondered the route for Asia in waters that
none in the world had seen before.
The men who died, we buried in this sea:
the carpenter, soldiers, sailors, a cooper.
At this time we believed the trend of our course
skirted northwesternmost America;
but sunless, we reckoned by guesswork only.
Squalls spun volumes of shadow above us.
We were forced to abide the enmity then
of the unimpeachable sea. Our pilot,
the ancient, trusted André Hesselberg,
revealed that in his seafaring life
he never encountered a storm so envious.
Hunks of wind hurled cannon shot
or lifted a keening soprano through
the whiplash of hail. Courage hid
from the lightning as it ricocheted, left
and right, uncurtaining chaos to
seconds of time, for mostly then
we moved without measure, with vision
blind even to the waves above and below.
Opinion was broken by doubt. Some begged
for retreat towards America; others rudely
defended the desperate onward track.
The storm tormented us with its sting

equally when it abated, and ice
stripped our faces. Once a rainbow
dared its arc before us, dipping
chromatic chords in the twofold ocean,
and we bound ourselves again to continue.
But hardly did breathing ease in the interval
than the gale attacked the air, undivided
in novel fury. The officers, fearing
capsize of the ship, advised a change
in the course, but the captain would not change.
His reckoning implied that we had reached
a spot some hundred miles from our port.
The *St. Peter* wallowed like driftwood, more
like a wreck than a ship. Then officers
stumbled to their posts, feet
slow to obey the will. Lieutenant
Waxel, sturdy Swede, sought for
words to waken the crew. He no longer
promised a sight of Kamchatka but said
"Trust in God and look for land —
any land, where we can find means to live
and so, to continue our voyage." November
the fourth, it was written in the log,
"By the will of God the Siberian soldier
Ivan Davidov died of scurvy."
But no man dies by the will of God
of scurvy. On that day also the sky
hinted a new dimension. Not land?
Our land? We had not raised the sextant
in the storm shroud, but dead reckoning

asked if this snowy wedge could be
the cape, Shipunski, near the harbour
from which we had sailed. At the cheerful guess
the ship came alive and stirred with the image;
the sick commander roused himself
and spoke of Asia and the end of starvation.
At noon the sun startled our eyes.
Waxel lifted the sextant; he read
and calculated the sign in the heaven,
plotting our place on the globe by angle
of solar height. And the word filtered
through the hesitant ship, that the latitude
lay too far to the North for Avacha,
the home port. Yet the pull of our wish
mapped in our minds some unknown headland
on Siberia's coast, in the lee of which
to anchor. Already we schemed to send
a courier running to Kamchatka post
for food and horses, to hurry rescue.

As these dreams blossomed, the sun
dipped down, and at night a new storm
barred our progress with frantic air
and volleys of water. No man in the crew
could reef the sails. The mainmast toppled.
Doubt led every mind to question
whether the weltering ship could survive.
Men and officers heard the summons
to Bering's cabin, where he lay ready
to command, though absent from the bridge

and actual maneuver of the ship. The few
who still could walk, a shrinking company,
entered his cabin for the council. They
debated at length, for the Captain Commander
urged that we hold the course for Avacha,
but he would not overrule the others.
Six casks of water remained. Of flour
some hundred pounds. But Lieutenant Waxel
and Fleetmaster Khitrov and I, the mate,
bore the burden of manning the ship.
Forty-five men lay in their bunks,
the rest, cripples too feeble to work.
We had to agree that the chance of life
depended on landing. The naturalist Steller
disagreed, but for once did not argue.
He said we had always rejected his word
on navigation. (And we had. And were right.)
Yet we couldn't deny his knowledge of science;
and it was disturbing to hear him say
this coast could be only another island.
By experience we knew no such thing
to be true. For on Bering's earlier voyage,
he found this region empty of islands
on his way North then to the Icy Cape
in search of the Northwest passage to China
or the joining of Russian and American soil.
And he had settled that question of the passage
forever, even if we failed, and of us
some had been with him then, through these waters.
Thus by vote the council concluded to land

with one dissent. The captain concurred
and gave the order. We steered for shore.
(It was not Steller who voted "no,"
but a surly officer, reduced in rank,
but he pitched in later and bore his part.)
In the night the moon exploded a warning,
a flare of silver on the bellowing surf.
About to breach! Some in astonishment
prayed, "Oh God our ship!" Others laughed
in anger. We lowered the anchors, but the cables
snapped. Amidst our confusion, rapidly
waves rove us over the reef
into the one inflection of the coast
where a ship could shelter. Thus we began
November, having held the sea for five months.

How can the slow translation to shore
be told to you ? Above the shingle,
snow hid the unfamiliar earth.
We saw no timber. Willow shrubs
one foot high and the width of a thumb
hatched the hollows. Useless for building.
We burrowed into the sand, to make
underground huts. Only Steller
and one or two others could do much work.
The sick lay out on the open beach,
until we could carry them into these dugouts.
It took two weeks to get all the company
on land. We existed in a state of nature
like the savage fellows of North America.

Over a small depression in the ground,
those who could walk put up a tent
for the Captain Commander. As sand sifted
into the hole, he lay half buried,
preferring the warmth. George Steller
collected pungent leaves for a salad
to cure the scurvy, and cooked some liver
of the sea otter, but Bering would not eat.
He fancied only the delicate ptarmigan
hunters had shot. Cheerful in speech,
the captain appeared to ignore his misery
and began to plan for the future of the crew.
He roused the constable, Roselius,
to scout along the shore to the North
and search for people. After six days
Roselius dragged himself back to the camp;
he had walked thirty miles. He saw nothing hopeful
no familiar terrain, no link with Kamchatka.
He uncovered no path and found no fire.
Then Bering summoned Steller to his tent
and asked him frankly to open his mind
about this region. Steller – he was opinionated
and critical of others, yet in his own way
he had skill – spoke respectfully: "Sir,
on the beach I stumbled upon a window
of poplar, carved with Russian design
probably from the dwellings near
the mouth of the river Kamchatka; and
I uncovered also a curious trap
for foxes. The teeth are not of iron

but made with shells. I think the current
drove this here from American shores,
for there is nothing so primitive used by
the Chukchi or Koriak tribes in Kamchatka.
Do we not notice how tamely, sir,
the wild animals wait, and passively
allow our approach ? They have never been hunted.
The plants and creatures do not differ
from the kinds I have studied on the peninsula
except for the curious beast, the sea cow.
Southward, midday clouds and sky
drink the opal colour of ocean.
We have not reached Russia." The captain did not
reveal his opinion, but he said
"The vessel can probably not be saved;
May God at least spare for some our long boat."

Vitus Bering, that Dane, had sailed twice to the Indies
before he enlisted in the Russian Navy
and served the Czar for forty years.
Because of his knowledge of the East, and his zeal,
the Naval Academy chose him to command
in our Muscovite bid for Pacific discovery.
This was his second expedition.
Ten years he had laboured preparing it,
beginning with the wearing overland struggle,
from St. Petersburg to Western Siberia.
Three years he worked in Yakutsk, building
vessels to carry the party up the Lena
to the Arctic. Furnace and foundry

rose, and they forged anchors and ironwork
in this wilderness, for the expected voyage
to America. Couriers ranged Siberia
for money, cloth, oil, hemp.
The Russian nobles ruling these posts
ignored Moscow, foul-mouthed
lazy exiles. And our learned republic
of scientists, compelled us to haul
nine wagon loads of their instruments,
and a library! They even demanded cabins
on the river boats. (But Yakutsk was too tough
for most of them, and they went home. Would to God
they had taken Professor de la Croyère
and his lying map that later misled us.)
Bering pushed on to Okhotsk.
For this, he furnished seventy river craft
and wharves, piers and docks for winter
(when we could not sail through ice). At Okhotsk
he and Spanberg constructed a village.
Spanberg sailed to Japan and returned.
Nine ships now rode in the harbour.
We had built them all, and the barracks, by the urging
of the persevering Dane. Under him we ferried
powder, cannon, hemp, canvas
from Yakutsk. Down the Lena, then up
the Aldan, the Maya, and Udoma. Across
the Stanovoi mountains. Down the Urak.
Walking the banks and pulling the barges.
Three years to transport the stores to Okhotsk.
Two years more before Bering could

sail to Kamchatka. The natives refused
our food and had to be driven by the whip.
(Some say Bering was too lenient
with them.) We ate their reindeer meat.
Already the commander suffered from fever.
He spoke his misgiving to a few of the officers.
He would have liked a younger man
and a Russian to take command for the final
voyage, but the duty was his.

                      His dying
concern in life was for the *St. Peter.*
He calmly ordered the able-bodied
to beach the ship and secure her with hawsers.
But only five could walk; they
and the Fleetmaster Khitrov could not summon
brawn sufficient to beach the *St. Peter.*
Again they beat at the walloping wind
but could not get out to her. Then the wind
itself did the work, drove her right on the beach
where we had intended. The storm saved the ship
from leaving us, but cracked the keel and the hull.
The water flooded the ship at high tide
and loaded her with sand as the tide ebbed,
proving the injured planks. But Bering
died before he appraised the damage.

He had filled an empty space on the chart
from the known West to the unknown East.
Aware of his final small discovery

of land, an island, he made no sign
in order not to discourage the crew.

Waxel the Swede, himself on the sick list,
assumed command. But we no longer
performed as disciplined men. Rank
didn't count in the fight to survive.
Forty men in five huts
learned to govern themselves by consent.
No one worked because ordered, or for money.
The precious sea otter skins had no value;
we hunted the animals only for meat.
We cared most for an awl or a kettle,
a shirt, a packet of needles or string,
like the simple Americans we had laughed at.
And the beached ship stood as our factory;
we salvaged every possible tool
but agreed not to eat the flour,
thinking ahead, to the voyage home.
Necessity drove each man upright
to take to the trades, and be carpenter, cook,
tailor, or hunter in his turn.
I kept the log in weeks that followed,
when I could thaw my stiffened fingers,
as the wheel of winter moved time forward.
The whimsical sea, our one-time enemy
bore us our only freight, herds of
sea-bears, from which we stripped the fat
and ate the stringy meat. Logs
of pine swam from America, riding

the miles we had buffeted. Flotsam of paddles
and planks of ships brought firewood
out of the sea, or gave us the means
of shoring our refugee camps in the sand.
Twice earthquakes caved their walls.
Vectors of wind flung us out
of the burrows. We had to roof them again
with wave-fretted wood that we dragged, like oxen
harnessed to a yoke, across rough miles.
Like prospectors, our eyes devoured
the ground, for when we lacked fuel,
we chewed the sinews of the otter raw.
Blue foxes (they were the only animals)
seized our clothes, our tools, our footgear
from the camp at night and robbed us
not only for food, but out of malice;
trivial demons, we hated them, but laughed
in spite of ourselves at their tricks.

We combed the island for food, and hid
from hail and snow in caves. We lived,
and winter retreated. But to rescue ourselves,
we had to discover our present place.
Roselius started in a new direction.
This time he doubled the cape to the North.
Ocean locked the land, all-encompassing,
as Steller predicted. And Bering knew.
We could not escape without a ship.
When men follow the sea or move
in a foreign element, some must understand

the construction of the vessel. Our carpenters had died.
The decision to break up the brig disunited us.
Many of the remaining crew argued
that the *St. Peter* could be repaired. Officers,
having surveyed the damage, denied this.
Finally everyone signed a paper
agreeing (lest we be criticized by
the government, later) to build a new
ship from the old. Out of the ranks
a Siberian laborer volunteered,
a man who had watched the building of ships
three years ago, in Okhotsk. He said
"If the Lieutenant will draw the plan
I believe I can build a ship so solid
that with God's help, we can put to sea in it."

Then we took to pieces the two-masted
brig, the *St. Peter,* buried in the shingle.
She was finished for sailing. We saved each timber,
all the canvas and part of the rigging.
It took three weeks of toil to dismantle her.
Meantime, incoming tides of spring
brought wood, like manna, to the beach, indispensable
for charcoal; without that fuel we could not
have worked a smithy. And we had to design
tools, to beat hammer and crowbar and wrench
from the salvage. But our strength increased amazingly,
for out of the sea appeared innocent monsters –
sea-cows, manati, swam in with the tide
to eat the celery in shore. We studied

ways to hunt them and, standing on rocks
nearby, speared them with improvised
harpoons. We throve on the unexpected
feasting, better than all the unsavoury
fare we first had to learn to swallow.
Now we steadied ourselves anew into discipline,
and when work lagged, with words of rescue
Lieutenant Waxel moved each man.
We divided ourselves into companies, one
hunting for us all, one setting up
supplies for the voyage, one joining together
the ship's timbers. Again skins
of the sea otter renewed old greed
and men gambled, hoping to return
rich, to Russia.

       In May we celebrated
when keel and stem and sternposts stood
erect. Waxel invented a drink
Mongolian style, blending grasses
with flour and train oil (for we had
no butter or tea), but it cheered us no less,
and we talked in his hut until midnight. Soon
the outer planks were curved into shape.
On shore a party laced the rigging;
but how to caulk the seams of our hooker
stopped us. We had no oakum. Then Waxel
fashioned a new apparatus. With rising
steam from a kettle, he melted tar
from bits of rope that had been stored

unused, on our former *St. Peter.* He then
shredded the rope and thickened the tar with it
to enseam the planks and seal out the sea.
Last, as the form of our saving labour
rose into visible fact, we dreaded
the gamble of launching, when all might be lost
if we could not slide the ship to the water
before a storm. But we contrived
a bilge block, and early in August, we
launched the hooker, stepped up the mast
and set the rigging. Each man ran
lightly; relief lifted our shoulders,
and we sang. Stowed the stores aboard, then
hung the rudder and bent on sails.
Three more days till we cheered the order,
"Weigh anchor!" Before we embarked,
we claimed the island for Russia and carved
a cross to mark it and honor Bering.
We rowed two miles to the outer sea,
and in the hooker *St. Peter,* born
of the old ship and rigged with her re-cut
sails, we reached our port, Avacha.
Kamchadal natives paddled out first,
welcome with news that the consort, *St. Paul,*
had returned the year before, under Chirikov.
A calm dissolved the silken water;
stars in their squadrons mapped the sky
above Asia. We entered the harbour, rowing.

A Note on *Yushin's Log*

Yushin's Log is an imagined narrative based on actual events. It has no one direct source; but the plan evolved itself some time after reading the documents printed in *Bering's Voyages, 2* vols., ed. by F. A. Golder (American Geographical Society, New York, 1922). This collection contains the brief log kept by the assistant navigator Kharlam Yushin, as well as the journal kept by the naturalist Georg Wilhelm Steller.

Bering's voyage from Kamchatka to Alaska took place in 1741.

JOHN LEDYARD'S VENTURE

A dream of Ledyard's venture came alive
on the Northwest coast of North America.
A corporal of marines on Captain Cook's ship,
the *Resolution*, he had sailed through
the Arcadia of sun-steeped islands scattered
in the South Pacific, enjoying like all the crew,
abundant fare of pork, yams, coconuts,
bread fruit, figs, bananas, a pleasure enhanced
by the all but naked dancing girls, poised
of posture, seductive in sex, and free to grant
their "favors" after the nightly feasting.
Elated by the subsequent finding,
in mid-Pacific, of hitherto unknown
islands, equally hospitable, Cook
named them for Lord Sandwich, but we
include them in the group we call Hawaiian.
Severe contrast in wind and temperature
as Cook progressed to the unexplored North
earned for their landfall on the Oregon coast
the name Cape Foulweather. Continuing,
the ships stood on and off the land until
the Commander found it safe to anchor,
where brown arms of earth embraced
quiet water. Ledyard, and all the sailors,
held little hope of meeting human beings
in this seeming void. But that very night
in blustery March, as he wrote in his journal,

out of nowhere appeared before them
"that hearty, that intrepid, that unique
and glorious creature, man." Silent statues
in smooth canoes moved close to the ship
and stayed immobile there until morning.
Cook quite naturally christened this
new-born place on the mappa mundi
"New Albion," the harbor, Nootka Sound.
Ledyard, after the distant years at sea
in a British ship, gazed at the continent
that gave him birth, two thousand miles
to the East, in New England, and as if he were
spellbound, at these still speechless people
dwelling on its Pacific coast. To him
they had to be fellow-Americans, kin
to the Indians of the Northeast he had met
and briefly lived with. Turning a page
he wrote, "The passions incident to
natural attachment and early prejudice soothed
a homesick heart. I was harmonized by this. . . ."
His youthful encounter was not accidental.
A beginning student at Dartmouth College
(founded to train missionaries as well as the Indians
they were meant to convert – hence the now
discarded name of its later football team) Ledyard
disappeared from the campus without leave
to live in the woods near the Canadian border
with one of the tribes of the Five Nations
and learn of their customs and some words
of their language. As the dugout canoes

of these imperturbable Pacific redskins
surrounded the British vessels – Cook's
and his consort, the *Discovery* – Ledyard
recalled his own, carved from a tree trunk
with the help of some classmates, transport
for his embryo voyage. A freshman dropout,
he sailed down the Connecticut to his foster home
in Hartford, the first white man to travel
so far on that rock-interrupted stream.
Now, at Nootka, he looked at copper bodies,
at painted faces, black hair brightened
with daubs of red and white, looked at beads
of wampum they wore. In a mind's flash
he conceived the whole continent unified
by trade, and whether or not he
was aware of it, an incentive ignited
that propelled his future. With wood and water
replenished, the vessels departed following
the compass needle northward in faithful search
for the elusive passage from East to West (or
was it the opposite?). Their Lordships
of the Admiralty handed Cook this chance
to complete his Michelangelesque cartoons
of Pacific cartography, with Sibylline figures
widening the aisles in the small human chapel
of our galaxy. Landing again and again
on the unidentified Alaskan coast, the seamen
met shorter, round-faced people. Ledyard
excitedly linked them with Labrador natives,
("Moony Eskimos" as the poet-geographer

Elizabeth Bishop called them). He inspected
nets, fish hooks, kayaks, paddles, sealskin
boots, fur garments, and – supreme marvel –
harpoons tipped with mussel shells for killing
Leviathan, the whale. The tools and instruments
of all these alleged savages, Ledyard mused,
showed an advance as far from man's beginnings
as Descartes or Newton from their historical base.
Frequently sent ashore in charge of the guard
to protect the men collecting wood and water,
Ledyard met these Eskimos north of Nootka,
where Cook, with his passion for accuracy,
profiled Prince William Sound (now fouled
by the Valdez). Everywhere the natives
traded briskly, pelts of softest fur
racoon, bear, sea otter, sealskin
bartered for just a knife or a piece of iron.
Once they caught the mariners unprepared
(this happened on a southward sweep, to the Pacific
sector studded by the Aleutian Islands).
An Indian canoe moved close to the *Discovery*,
signaled for a rope to be lowered, and attached to it
a box of bark. Opening this woody parcel
the officers found pieces of European paper
covered with letters no one could decipher.
Cook on the *Resolution* had never seen
anything similar but rightly guessed the language
might be Russian. He decided not to halt.
But some of the crew angered by his refusal
to search for possible shipwreck victims,

blamed him for the hair-raising experience
when the two ships, fog-blinded,
could communicate only by firing their guns,
and Cook had to command them to anchor
for a night of anxiety, until next day
a clearing sky unveiled the surrounding rocks,
a reef ready to annihilate them
had they deviated the smallest fraction from
their chosen course. They christened the island
Providence. Old hands recalled the legend
that Cook could smell the land.

For more than a month of hard-hauled sailing
past craggy cliffs, snow-scaped
mountains, smoking volcanoes, he led
northeast, with instruments on sky watch
charting this newest of new-found lands.
The sailors applauded the relative cleanliness
of the women here (compared to those at Nootka,
whom they had to immerse in tubs of hot water
before they could sleep with them).
Although the price of their "favors"
amounted to little more than a leaf of tobacco,
crew members did not skimp their rewards.
These were the people of Norton Sound, en route
to the "westernmost part of America hitherto known"
that Cook taught the map to label "Cape Prince
of Wales." Then he steered for a bay in Siberia
where he parleyed briefly with the unfriendly Chukchi,
who mistook him for their Russian overlords.

Through a narrow strait he advanced with rising hope
of finding an open sea that topped the globe
and could carry him back to Europe. Land appeared
to trend away both to the Northeast
and to the Northwest; some fervently started
to compute the distance to Baffin's Bay. But
when clearer weather allowed an accurate fix
of their position, four degrees above
the Arctic Circle on August 17,
a strange brightness tightened the afternoon sky,
signalling "ice blink" to the commander. No
novice in polar waters, Cook had explored
in the Antarctic on his second voyage
farther south than anyone before him,
leading the way, if you like, for Moby Dick,
Amundsen, Scott, Byrd, and the ozone hole.
The two ships pursued their progress to
the collage of ice floes pasted on the water,
until the sea rose up in its entire self,
frozen, to say, "Thou shalt not pass!"
Cook never fought with facts, nor failed
to verify their jurisdiction. A wall
twelve feet high, defied him
in this theater of cruelty, and worse than that,
the wall moved. It came towards them, propelling
its fringe of pieces above and below water
sharp enough to rip a keel. Ledyard,
unskilled in navigation, had no insight
into the decision-making process here;
however, from talk overheard of the junior officers,

he learned of Cook's compelling faith: if
balked of his original prize, with equal zeal
he set himself to go on learning
"how to improve geography and navigation."
And improve it he did. Alternately sailing
to the Russian or to the American shore, as gales
permitted, he sought a harbor where he might
recruit supplies – but with no luck. Instead
he directed men to hunt the "seahorse"
(i.e. walrus) draped on the ice floes.
An insomniac sun shone its lantern,
no spotlight, on the men in the small boats,
Ledyard with them in the pinching cold. He laughed
at the loud variety of obscene and blasphemous oaths
when they were ordered to eat the blubbery flesh.
Cook, himself in a small boat to examine
the ice enemy, also shot a walrus for himself;
and pioneer in saving his crew from scurvy, he
ate his share publicly, as he had earlier overcome
resistance to spruce beer and sauerkraut.
Twelve days in the ice; with amazed eye
Ledyard gawked at the long, lumbering, wedge-
headed polar bear, the Arctic fox
trotting across the floes with a puffin's egg
in its mouth to feed its pups, and he joined
in the universal joy when orders came to steer
southward. Cook had resolved not to risk
the safety of men and ships any longer.
He would winter in the Sandwich Islands,
and now that he knew the way, he could return

in the spring next year with a better chance.
They sailed again through the slender strait that
"in justice to Bering," Cook named for him.
Ledyard wrote in his journal, "We had the pleasure
to see both continents at once."
And the rhythm of his dream began to dance
the intercontinental. Cook had proved
that Alaska was part of the mainland,
not an island, and corrected more errors
on the maps he had had to rely on, during
the extra days he devoted to Norton Sound
(naming it for the Speaker of the House of Commons).
Here was no harbor to repair the *Resolution*'s
persistent leak; better to resort to
their old harbor on Providence, later given
the Indian name of Unalaska. Mystery
coheres in chance. Hardly had carpenters
landed to reshape sheathing, and smiths
set up their forge to make hatchets from
a bower anchor for the Hawaiian trade,
when an Indian chief, called Derramoush
challenged Cook with an innovative gift.
He brought a loaf of rye bread, baked
like a pie, filled with fresh salmon
seasoned with salt and pepper. Adept
in sign language, his eloquent hands, his
imagist drawings, portrayed a ship like theirs
bringing white men, who now inhabited
this island, and had dispatched him
to invite the strangers to their headquarters.

Cook would not send a group of men
to a potential enemy; from the ready line
of called-for volunteers Ledyard emerged
as chosen emissary, recommended
by his fellow countryman, Lieutenant Gore
– vital rapport in remote Pacific waters
between New England and Virginia,
which even then unknown to either man
gave pulse to the American Revolution.
The Yankee accepted Cook's command to go
with Derramoush wherever he might lead,
and return within a week; if he could not,
the ships would wait another week, then leave.
Unarmed, except for bottles of rum and brandy,
Ledyard kept up with Derramoush all day.
As the sky sombered, it disclosed a huddle
of grass-thatched huts sunk in the ground.
The Indians crowded round, quick to inspect
the visitor, but not with the shock of unbelief
of those who had never met a white man.
They didn't tear open his shirt or rub his skin.
Reassured, Ledyard descended the ladder
into one of the huts. Without ado
the women regaled him with dried fish,
and when Derramoush permitted, rushed to share
the white man's liquor. Fatigue offset
the vile odors of the dwelling. He slept.
At dawn a different chief shook him awake.
Less apprehensive than at first, his journal
tells us, Ledyard hiked over hilly, rough ground

in drenching rain with this Chief, Perpheela.
"Before the late sunset, we reached the shore
of an ocean bay. Perpheela loaded our luggage
in his waiting canoe, and transferred me
to another pair of natives. Ignorant
of my destination, I had no choice
but to go with them about six miles
along the bay, where we spied the vessel
furnished by Perpheela. With forceful gestures,
ominous in the oncoming night, the guides
demanded that I go down into the space
between the two holes where they would sit
to paddle. At first I refused. Doubt
assailed me: to bury myself
where I couldn't see, couldn't jump out
in case of danger? But it was all
or nothing. Once below, I heard and felt
the water sliding past my passive limbs.
After perhaps an hour, a sudden jolt
jarred my spine, above the sandy sound
of the canoe's beaching. Forcep arms
delivered me; alien syllables
like no known language, came
from fair-skinned giants, who had to be
the presupposed Russians. Unconsciously
a flow of energy entered my being
and flexed my muscles as I walked the path
by the golden lamps of my guides. They
released me to climb into a long hut.
Indians sat on the benches lining the walls,

and the Russians ahead, after more gibberish
of greeting and command, lost no time
in stripping my shivering body.
They pulled on a dry shirt, drawers,
and believe it or not, a fur cap, that pleased me
beyond measure. My guides had brought in
the package of liquor, allowing me to respond
to their kindness. On the shaky table before me
I lined up bottles of rum and brandy, plus
some good tobacco. They gathered
like a flock of birds and seemed to grasp the signs
I improvised to say that a great commander,
whom I served, made these gifts.
Right away, they turned me round, pointing
to a smoky portrait of a much-bejewelled,
richly-costumed lady, and bowed as if
with pride in her power. This had to be
their empress, Catherine the Great. Glasses
raised to her image, they toped our rum
before and after a briny feast: whale,
halibut boiled in oil, and fortunately
some broiled salmon, and thick black bread,
the only things I could swallow." Afterward
lying on one of the benches, in a bear skin,
he listened to the low-toned prayers
chanted by the Russians, as the Indians,
holding up tiny crucifixes, grunted in unison.
Religion is not mimicry, he mused,
drifting off to sleep in his fur cocoon.
No marine training prepared for the morning.

In the nearby hut where he was taken to bathe, stifled
by the steam that hissed from cauldrons over the furnace,
he fainted. Revived, he stretched out like the others,
naked as all were, on the platforms, under
doses of cool, cold, colder, coldest
jets of water. At breakfast, the smell of whale,
bear, and walrus turned his stomach. He begged
for a little dried salmon, and as soon as he could
he urged a return to the ship. But it was snowing,
and they would not budge. To make good use
of the time, Ledyard scribbled down as many words
as the Asiatic Indians would teach him.
He embarked with the Russians next day to take
a shorter route by boat across the bay.
With several of them in tow, he surprised
his Commander arriving before dark,
followed by Ismailov, factor of the Russian fur trade.
Praise from his captain, and the admiration
of all aboard the two ships, visibly
moved the romantic heart of Ledyard. Then
he stepped down to his modest rank of corporal.
He played no part in the eager exchange
of charts and maps between Cook and Ismailov.
"I was mortified," Cook said, "that I
could converse with him only by signs and figures."
Ismailov had once sailed in a French ship from
China to France, without learning the commonest words
like bread or wine. But he was well versed
in navigation and quickly crossed out
non-existent islands on earlier maps

of the Aleutians. And recent manuscripts
he kindly lent gave needed proof
that after Bering none of the Russians discovered
anything of moment on the North American coast.
Condensing his own, unchallenged findings
in a letter to the Admiralty, Cook then
trusted Ismailov to transmit it to London via
Kamchatka and Moscow. Then he called back
the men being entertained by the Russians,
and the ships weighed anchor for the Sandwich Islands.
To the satellite viewer, this lap of the voyage offers
a study in comedy. En route to Kauai, sailors
chorused "There is nothing like a wench!"
This was the island where, a year ago,
the more than willing Hawaiian women "rose
like Venus from the sea," as the susceptible surgeon
Samwell said. In spite of November gales,
they saw the island in a month, only
to have their vision of Arcadia fade.
Why would Cook not land to trade as usual?
Why forbid the women to come on board?
He kept his counsel, tacking on and off
for agonizing weeks. As he expected,
extra islands added themselves to the chart,
notably Maui. Here the natives nervously
hoisted an old man up the side of the ship,
their chief, Kirreaboo. He soon conferred on Cook
a beautiful feathered cloak, black and yellow.
With no premonition of future events that
were to link them indissolubly,

the two could talk together in friendly fashion
the lingo in these islands much the same
as in Tahiti or Tongataboo. The attempt
to persuade Cook to land on Maui failed
to deflect him from his southward course.
The chief withdrew, and the *Resolution* sailing
in due direction suddenly brought in view
a high, snow-capped mountain cresting
their major find, "Owhyhee,"
in native tongue. True to his imperatives
as explorer, Cook plied to windward,
seeking its eastern bounds. Ledyard, for once,
shared the resentment of semi-mutinous seamen.
Hauling tattered sails with crumbling rigging,
bone-tired, furious when given
sugar-cane beer instead of grog
and scanty fare in sight of a land of plenty
(Cook was saving liquor for the Arctic return,
keeping up the price of his iron,
and trying to protect the women from VD),
they kept on into January. At last,
when heaving the lead spelled safety
in a wide west side bay, Cook
adopted this anchorage, declaring a truce
with the waves for perhaps a two-week stay.
Word of mouth had scooped their arrival.
Hawaii's welcome startled Western eyes.
Aloft, officers counted the packed canoes
— at least a thousand. Hundreds of people swam
toward the ships like shoals of fish, and more

of every age, clapping and dancing, crowded
the beach, the housetops, branches of trees.
"God of creation, these are thy doings!
These are our brothers and our sisters,"
Ledyard exclaimed. So many climbed aboard
that the *Discovery* heeled over, and only a chief
Parea, saved the day by driving the surplus,
especially the women, overboard.
Another VIP, who seemed a priest,
accosted Cook, with presents of pigs and coconuts,
then bundled him up in red cloth,
"Koa," by name, intoning with a helper
mystifying phrases. Afterwards
all stayed to dine. Ledyard, of course,
was not one of the small party in the barge
that ferried Cook, Lieutenant King, and Bayley,
the astronomer, to shore. They alone
witnessed the amazing apotheosis.
Waving white wands, the escorting chief
cried above the water, "Make room!
The great Lono comes!" Whereat
the canoeing natives all abased themselves.
Landing on the beach at Karrakakooa
(to English ears), the arch priest Koa
grabbed Cook's hand; again the chiefs,
waving their wands, announcing "Lono! Lono!"
opened a path through the multitude.
The people fell prostrate, and hid their faces
— only to follow crawling on hands and knees —
as Cook walked rapidly forward, having

collided with a myth. As the leader reached
a sacred precinct (recognized by the English
from the South sea sojourn as a morai),
they went through a railing topped by human skulls.
At the far end, a rickety scaffold
topped the paved enclosure, within a circle
of wooden images. Cook allowed the priest
to lead him to the scaffold, and stood there
impassive, while Koa lifted
a rotting hog and chanted syllables,
then dropped it on something like an altar.
Endless trivia of ritual, Cook seated
in state, again the red cloth wrapping;
procession with an edible hog, parades
of the select Hawaiians to their images,
addresses sacred and profane (in manner,
for the language varied too much from everyday);
speed-up chants between priests,
the climax "Lono! Lono!" Even anointing.
Cook was not one to relish flattery.
In every clime he complied with custom
as a matter of policy. It was part of his job
to report what he could of native religion.
Feasting was part of it. He looked askance
in spite of himself, when Koa offered pieces
of the fresh-roasted hog with the same hands
that had uplifted the tainted one; worse
when the priest then chewed it for him.
The time came to wind up the affair,
with the presence of "Eatooa," their god.

Meanwhile the commander's practiced eye
spied an adjoining sweet potato patch
suitable for an observatory – no doubt
with this in mind he had chosen the astronomer
of the *Discovery*, Bayley, to come with him.
He struck a price with the Hawaiians, agreeing
also to let them plant white wands
about the area, to be taboo for natives
and out of bounds for the English after dark.
Under Lieutenant Phillips, Corporal Ledyard
had charge of marines to guard this enclosure
and set up the marquee for the instruments,
always landed for accurate calculation.
For him, a student of people rather than stars,
it functioned like a duck blind.
Lieutenant King responsible for activities
on-shore, reported the strange symptoms
of veneration for Cook. He couldn't
take a step without the preceding
priests, the white wands, the echoing cry
of "Lono! Lono!" and villagers tumbling down
before him, chiefs winding him
in red cloth as he came to visit the huts
and gazing upon him with awe all through
the inescapable feasting. Yet on the ships
they did as they pleased, swapping their
pigs and breadfruit or coconuts
for a piece of iron, stealing whatever they could
while the women sold themselves to the sailors.
But Ledyard saw the seeds of conflict

growing in the tabooed ground of the observatory.
The men in the ranks felt they were cheated
of the sexual adventures their shipmates enjoyed.
A few officers stole out at night
to meet their "mistresses" on neutral ground.
Of course the rank and file soon knew.
"To deny them," Ledyard wrote, "was to oppose
passions which could pervade stone walls."
The white wands went down, angering
the neighboring priests by this betrayal
of a covenant. But Cook could not attend
to a minor problem. For the past two days
no canoes had come with food for the ships.
A taboo on traffic had completely emptied the bay
to dignify the impending advent
of King Kirreeaboo. War canoes
seventy-feet long, sails aloft,
carrying feather-clad idols, conveyed
the king and queen and royal retinue.
Cook almost failed to recognize the man
who came aboard in full regalia, plumed
helmet and scarlet cloak, as the same feeble
Kirreeaboo who had been an inquisitive
visitor to his ship at Maui. Now
it was friendship at second sight for both.
Kirreeaboo gave Cook a royal helmet
and cloak in prismatic color like his own.
Cook bestowed shining knives and hatchets.
They exchanged names, then in the cabin
feasted with every mark of ceremony

where a high priest, Koa, new
to the English, made up for the king's
restricting himself to breadfruit and water
by cramming himself with pork and fowl. Later
they learned their debt to the man they termed
"the Bishop." That night the royal party went
back to Kiverua at the northern end of the bay.
Next day Kirreeaboo set forth in state
with high priest Koa and basket images
made of red, black, and yellow feathers,
with eyes of oyster shells, and distorted mouths.
On they came singing in their canoes,
and landed without notice at the observatory.
Ledyard headed the honor guard hastily
assembled; Cook hurried over from the *Resolution*
in his pinnace, to receive in the marquee
the beautiful cloak Kirreeaboo gracefully
threw over him. After the ceremonies,
Kirreeaboo asked them to tell him
the reason for the observatory. He came
to question but stayed to wonder. The astronomer,
Bayley, did his best to demonstrate
the instruments, Cook to explain their use
at sea. But it was too soon for such
a technological broad jump across
diverse cultural time zones. The tall
telescopes frightened the king; quadrants
seemed to hold magic in metal. Ledyard
listened to the shaken king's conclusion:
if watching by day and night the motions of the sun,

the moon, and the stars, could guide us
over many oceans, we ourselves
must be descendents of the heavens.
As January ended, events traveled
fast forward. The *Resolution*'s rudder
went on shore for repair, carpenters
cut plank from inland trees, aided
by Koa's gifts of food. Hard to believe
that after that the English chopped down
the railing of the Morai, including some of the images,
for firewood. Ledyard was horrified.
A hankering Ledyard had for another adventure
Cook approved, and with Vancouver of fame
to come, a small party attempted to climb
Mauna Loa, the snowy volcano.
Unable to reach the top, Ledyard was back
in time to enjoy the festive Hawaiian games
of boxing and wrestling the English had requested,
and the brown bodies dancing, dancing, dancing
to the drums, their only music. They hooted
with laughter at our high-pitched violin,
but the flute beguiled them, and they swayed
easily to the sensuous tones of the French horn
playing them home, over the water.
Cook chose to entertain the king
with a display of fireworks. A huge crowd
waited all day until after dark,
and when they were silent as the night a sudden
thunder split the sky apart and rained down
bright golden arrows. The astonished

natives took to their heels, fled to the hills
or jumped into the water, but Kirreeaboo,
quivering, held his ground and recalled them.
He conducted himself at all times, Ledyard
noted, as a ruler worthy of his people.
He did not disguise his anxiety
about the date of Cook's departure.
The lesser chiefs resorted to signs, stroking
the sides and patting the sleek bellies of the sailors
in contrast to their own. Two hundred
hungry men had lived on the land; stores
of pork, breadfruit, yams, coconuts
loaded the ships with a six-months' supply.
Daring thefts by the natives multiplied –
like that of the pewter plate and cutlery
stolen from Lieutenant King while he slept.
But he used diplomacy rather than punishment
and praised the "friendly and happy" relationship
with the Hawaiians as a warrant to the English of safety
during their short stay on the island, home
to perhaps 100,000 people. A climax
of gift-giving marked the final days.
As the host at his house, Koa handed over
to Kirreeaboo hatchets and other iron
obtained from the English. The well-pleased monarch
gave Cook a shining pile of feathers,
cloaks, and cloth, and a royal larder of pigs,
plantains, pineapples, yams, and coconuts
 – more wealth than even Tahiti
or Tongataboo had bestowed. Cook

gave much of the food to the common people
from whom it had been requisitioned the night
before — the very people who guided
the ship's carpenters over a difficult road
and helped to carry the timber, refusing pay.
Now the observatory went on board,
and early in the morning, February 4th,
1779, the ships departed. With the course
set hopefully for the north, they
hugged the shore enroute to Maui, a source
of water fresher than the brackish kind at Hawaii.
But winds favor no human purpose. Only
a few days out a would-be hurricane
ripped the sails and ruined the foremast.
If he could have conjured a nearby harbor, Cook
would have done it. He loathed the thought
of revisiting Karrakakooa, and the crew
dammed the foremast. But the case for survival
dictated retreat. They took time
to rescue natives from capsized canoes
as gales intensified. Back at the old
anchorage, a déjà vu set in
with an awareness of being unwelcome. A vacant
bay, no clapping or singing, no traders eager
to bargain. "Cook was chagrined," Ledyard said.
Yet not a moment was lost in getting the mast
on shore, and he again had a share in the task
of guarding the carpenters and the observatory
near the Morai. Kirreeaboo came
to visit the ships and lift the taboo on trade

but did not disguise his displeasure at their return.
One episode after another revealed
Hawaiian hostility. Asked to help,
they replied with stone-throwing, until
confronted with an armed marine. Lieutenant King
heard with dismay Cook's new order
to fire with bullets rather than small shot
at the offenders. Ledyard was with him
when he joined Cook in running along the shore
in unsuccessful pursuit of the thieves who had stolen
the invaluable armorer's tongs from the *Discovery*.
In going on board the *Resolution*, the Captain
expressed his sorrow that he would have to use force
if the Hawaiians hindered the expedition,
and he turned all the women and others out of the ship.
At daybreak that mortal morning Lieutenant King
reported to Cook as planned, only to hear
of a far more frightening theft: overnight
the large cutter of the *Discovery* had been taken.
It had been moored underwater at the stern of the ship.
Clerke, in declining health from tuberculosis,
could not execute Cook's plan
to land with an armed guard at Kiverua
and persuade Kirreeaboo to come on board
for a visit – in effect to be a hostage
until the cutter was returned. Small boats
were to seal off the bay at each end.
Steering south to his post near Karrakakooa,
whatever his foreboding, Lieutenant King
welcomed the assignment of calming the fears of the natives.

He ordered the marines to stay in the marquee,
arms at the ready, but refused a request
from Ledyard to test-fire his loaded musket.
He then conferred with old Koa and the priests,
explaining that Cook was angry only with those
who stole the cutter, and peaceful men
would not be harmed. Inside the observatory,
he again employed himself in the contradictory
taking of altitudes, events elsewhere unseen.
Cook, with Lieutenant Phillips and nine marines,
landed at Kiverua. At the monarch's house
Phillips, entering to tell him of Cook's arrival
found their old acquaintance barely awake.
After talking with him the Captain concluded
that Kirreeaboo had no part in the scheme
to steal the cutter. He readily agreed
to go with them, and they were progressing
toward the boats, when an old woman in tears,
one of his wives, stopped him, and chiefs
laid hold of him, forcing him to sit down.
Cook's party sensed for the first time now
the angry mood of the two or three
thousand people surrounding them.
With Cook's approval Phillips lined the marines
along the rocks at the water's edge, and the crowd
made way, without ceasing to gather
stones and spears. Some had the iron spikes
they called pahooahs, bought from the English.
Notwithstanding a priest singing to him,
offering a coconut, Cook told Phillips,

"We cannot compel their king to go on board
without killing a number of these people."
Before he could change his plan, a nearby native
lunged at him with a spear and lofted a stone.
Cook's quick discharge of small shot
did not pierce the mats they wore as a shield.
At once a chief tried to stab Phillips,
who staved him off with the end of his musket.
A fury of stone-throwing followed. A Marine
was knocked down. Cook fired a ball
and killed a man. After ordering the marines
to fire, he called out "Take to the boats!"
Phillips repeated the order and fired just after
the Captain. Knocked down by a stone, and stabbed
in the shoulder as he rose, he shot his assailant dead,
amazed that the natives had not yet retreated,
their shouts and yells adding to the assault.
Only the fire from a boat offshore afforded
a chance for a few to escape. Phillips himself
lost sight of Cook and scrambled into the water.
After reaching the pinnace, he jumped overboard
in spite of his wounds, to save a man from drowning.
Captain Cook got to the water's edge.
The men in the pinnace saw him waving his hat.
To signal a cease fire? Or to come in?
A chief behind him stabbed him in the shoulder
or back of his neck. He staggered and fell forward
into the tide. A great shout exploded.
Hundreds rushed to join in stabbing and stoning
Lono, the god ungodded and destroyed.

With him died three marines and Corporal Thomas.
On the *Discovery* Captain Clerke, disturbed
by the volley of small arms, the violent
shouting, viewed through his field glasses
their people being driven off from the shore.
The *Resolution*, nearer to them, threw
shot from her cannon into the throng of natives.
The time was about 8:00 a.m.
At Karakakooa more than a mile away
the sound of musketry and the great guns
so agitated King that he abandoned
all effort to take altitudes.
Ledyard, with him, deplored the misguided
impact of the *Discovery*'s four-pounders,
which scared the women and children on the wall
and undercut King's promise of their safety.
The firing ceased and waiting without word
tightened the torment. Then the remaining cutter
approached, with Mr. Bligh's terse command
"Strike the observatory as soon as you can!"
Before he could voice the annihilating fact
that Cook was dead, they saw it
writ large in the look of him and the sailors.
These men now joined the marines in the job
of dismantling the astronomical tents
and repulsing stone-throwing Hawaiians.
Fresh orders came with a muster of men
– everyone in both ships who could fire a gun –
to protect the carpenters and to maneuver the mast
into the water. The violent skirmishes ended

when King arranged a cease-fire with the priests
and they could debark, towing the vital timber.
Back on the *Resolution* before noon
Ledyard witnessed discipline reshaping
the chain of command. Clerke replaced Cook
as Commodore; Lieutenant Gore rose
to be Captain of the *Discovery*. The ailing Clerke
did not flinch from the colossal challenge
he could not have foreseen. Benumbing grief
that silenced every soul on the ship all morning
gave way to a hubbub of cries for revenge.
Clerke sifted opinions from his staff.
But he had prayed, and his paramount aim
governed: to persevere in the given assignment
and sail again to the north in search of a passage.
He stifled his own desire for stern reprisal.
Loss of manpower he must not risk
by landing in force to destroy Kiverua.
About four that afternoon Lieutenant King
in the pinnace, flying a white jack in the stern,
advanced at the head of two small boats
of well-armed men, Ledyard among them.
King was ordered to stay offshore and parley
with the natives for the return of Cook's body and those
of the four marines. The sight of the white flag
brought people down from the hills with a roar
of satisfaction. Men threw off the mats
they wore as shields, women reached out
in gestures of friendship. Koa the priest
swam out to the pinnace. Naming himself

"Britannee" he offered King a pig
and begged for a piece of iron. King avoided
his tearful embrace and laid a cautious hand
over his dagger. He had never trusted the man
but when "Britannee" promised to bring him
Cook's body, there had to be hope.
And now the two-mindedness began
of the inhabitants and the arrivers,
of each within itself and toward the other.
In the small boats they heard a different story.
Closer to shore, natives told sailors
Cook's body had been cut to pieces
and carried a long way off. They seemed pleased
by what they had done. Only the flag of truce
and Clerke's new order to return restrained
King from destroying them. As they rowed
back to the ship, a Hawaiian on a rock
bared his backside in contempt, and Burney
had to strike the gun from King's hand.
Well after dark the next night, a canoe
neared the ship; a shot from the guards
brought a roar of "Tinnee! Tinnee!", their name
for King (whom they believed to be the son
and successor of Cook). The men in the canoe
swore they were friends and had something to give them.
Allowed on deck, their fear subsided, they wept
for the loss of Lono; King recognized one
as the priest Kairekeea, the "taboo man"
who had always marched before Cook with his wand.
He said that the bundle under his arm contained

a part of Lono. Unwrapping it,
Clerke found a heavy piece of flesh,
six or seven pounds cut from the thigh.
Distraction and madness struck every mind
at the horrible sight. Kairekeea said
most of the body had been burned, but Koa
had saved this part for them. Kirreeaboo
had kept the bones and the head for himself.
Clerke and King trusted Koa, "the bishop,"
and knew this man and other priests as friends.
He was forthright in reporting that now Kirreeaboo
and all his people were their mortal enemies,
"Britannee" a spy, his attempts to decoy King
on land a plot to get rid of him.
He would not agree to stay overnight.
As soon as his companion's wound was dressed
he said they must go; then both
astounded their hosts with anxious questioning.
When would Lono come back to Hawaii?
And what would he do to them? Fearful
but friendly, they paddled away in the secret dark.
Ledyard witnessed none of this first-hand.
Hearsay held the natives to be cannibals.
He was in the forefront of the effort to meet
the absolute imperative, to water the ships
from the only available well, near the Morai.
From the start the natives opposed them,
launching a storm of stones from behind the walls,
and badly wounding some of the seamen. Therefore,
the next time all the available men, armed

with pistols, cutlasses, hand grenades, bayonets,
marched in a column through Karakakooa.
The people fell on them with spears, daggers, stones,
inflicting casualties and making work impossible.
Then before an officer could stop them
some of the watering party set fire
to the houses nearest the well, and it spread
to the northeast part of the village. No mercy was shown
to the refugees. Yet all this time the women
on board the ships showed no desire to leave,
and a few swam out each day to be with the crewmen.

       Concurrently, the carpenters repaired the mast;
others worked on the rigging. Ledyard believed
the watering party would not again be molested.
But now from the top of a steep hill the natives
hurled down huge rocks upon them.
At that, undisciplined men, teeming with fury
at the treatment of Cook, ran wild; they killed
some of those hiding in a house, beheaded two,
fixed the heads on a pole and displayed them
to the opponents above. Lieutenant King
(the only officer who might have prevented brutality),
confined to the *Resolution* by minor surgery,
he – who had studied at Oxford and the Sorbonne,
and was a friend of Edmund Burke – had to
ask himself, Who is the savage here?
Suddenly there was a lull; his eye
caught an extraordinary sight, of children
coming down the hill with green boughs,

fluttering white flags, a man in the lead,
who proved to be their benevolent friend
Kairekeea. Received on board by Clerke
he brought an urgent message from Kirreeaboo
of his desire for peace. Warmly welcoming
the offer and the emissary, Clerke said
peace would be real between them only when
Kirreeaboo surrendered the bones of the Captain.
After an interval a chief Hiapo
brought word of agreement. Clerke in the pinnace
and King in the cutter went toward the shore
where Hiapo stood with presents of hogs, yams,
and the usual largesse. Taken to the ship
he gave them a bundle carefully wrapped in a cloak
of black and white feathers. In it they found
most of Cook's skull, his scalp, his hands.
Clerke looked at the hands. They had been scored
and salted. He knew them well. This was his third
voyage with Cook. He recognized the scar
on the right one, from an exploding powder horn
on the Newfoundland coast, years ago.
On two more days Hiapo came with a few
remaining bones and presents from Kirreeaboo.
He said he could not satisfy Clerke's request
for the other bodies, disbursed among various chiefs.

     All hands kept busy about the rigging.
Ledyard was always on shore with the watering parties
completing their job. Hogs and fruit
were traded without danger, and Clerke sent

Kirreeaboo a red cloth cloak
he had asked for before (as Clerke put it)
"this miserable breach." On the twentieth
they stepped the foremast, not without risk
when the purchase gave way several times.
Clerke then had Hiapo taboo the bay.
The immortal words of the service were spoken.
With flags flying half-mast the *Resolution*
tolled her bell and fired four-pounders.
The remains of Captain Cook in a homely coffin
sank into the ocean that he had made into a path
to knowledge of far-out encounters with the land
and the polarities of people on its borders.
As the sky darkened, a light breeze blowing
offshore, the two ships unmoored
and sailed out of the bay, bound for Kamchatka.

The wind sighed and moaned down the suffering sails,
as they struggled to reach the Northwest passage
for more than a month. Ledyard did not need
an officer's perspective to perceive the pull of necessity.
Food ran low. "The honest fellows," as Clerke
called them, pumped and bailed the leaking ships
from dawn to dark, now pinched by the cold
in their thread-bare clothing and shoeless feet
after the broiling sun of Hawaii. In a storm
the *Resolution* lost sight of her consort.
Snow masked land and mountains as they moored
in what seemed, and proved to be, the bay of Avacha
near Petropavlosk. This was Bering's point of departure

on his voyage of discovery to Northwest America.
They gazed at the shore, barricaded by ice,
at the squat log huts, and the conical ones built
on stilts, about a mile away. Soon
a small party headed by a Russian sergeant
drew up on the ice to oppose their landing, never
having seen a sizable ship before, and frightened.
Sign language didn't work, but luckily
the draughtsman, Webber, employed to sketch the voyage
knew German, and the sergeant could understand
a little. The ones whom he invited to his hut
(and fed with fish, game, and huckleberries)
hurried back with news of a Major Behm,
commandant of the district with headquarters
fifty miles away on the Sea of Okhutsk.
Despatches to him evoked a kind reply;
to acquaint him with their needs Captain Gore,
Lieutenant King, and German-speaking Webber
sped across the snow-paved ground
in sledges drawn by speedy dogs. In the interval
Russian and Polish merchants licensed by the Empress
to trade for furs, snapped up any of their
sea otter or beaver, to the profit of the crew.
Eleven guns saluted Major Behm,
arrived to visit Commodore Clerke.
He provided them with cattle, tar, canvas,
rye meal, tea, and tobacco, and refused
to accept compensation, since the Empress
he said, would prefer him to answer all their needs.
He left, entrusted with Cook's journal, and faithfully

forwarded it to St. Petersburg for transmission
to London. In Russia, King wrote, "We met
with feelings of humanity which would have done honor
to any nation or climate." A flicker of fantasy
crossed Ledyard's mind as to Catherine's benevolence.
With resources renewed, the two ships unmoored,
and as they waited for a favoring wind, the volcano St. Paul
that bore to the north and west on the bay of Avacha,
signaled a link with Bering. The sky darkened,
the atmosphere flamed. A shower of ashes
and sulphurous-smelling mud covered the decks;
thunder and lightning burst forth, until
next day a lively breeze shot them out
to sea. With Clerke, their fatally ill commander,
resolved to fulfill Cook's mission in searching
for a Northwest Passage between the oceans,
they pressed for the Arctic, along the fog-ridden
coast of Siberia. Ledyard could never forget
the earlier time when going through Bering's strait
he could see Russia and America simultaneously.
A tingling of the mind and body seized him
so strongly, that he could not stop to ask, What cause?
or even wish to. A seed of hope was planted.
This time he did not comment. In early July
the phantasmagoria of ice began. Loose slats
of frozen water impeded their way at once.
Ledyard knew little of navigation; he
could not see the point of apparent waffling
between two continents as Clerke doggedly
tried to follow Cook's plan, to trace

the American coast farther than the year before,
but the solid ice blocked them in headless towers
high above the dark-sailed vessels.
With no choice but to explore its boundaries
Clerke turned westward toward Asia.
When they came to occasional open pools, he ordered
the small boats out with parties prepared to shoot
walrus, or "seahorse" as the crew christened
the hated fare. Ledyard was only one of the hands
to hunt and consume it, and cut up the blubber
for lamp oil. Late in July, they aimed
successfully at a polar bear, for whom
the Arctic was named by the Greeks (our Great Dipper
pointing north was *Arctus,* their Great Bear).
This one meant hundreds of pounds of meat
"palatable and wholesome," Clerke held
in the last entry he jotted down in his journal.
Yet the relief was momentary. Tired
of raising and lowering the ice anchors, luffing
sails in the frigid air, the crews lost
the will to work even for their own safety.
It was touch and go for survival. A council of officers
met; decision and destiny concurred
and said "Go!" They steered southeast.
Late in August Ledyard watched the jolly boat
going to the *Discovery,* to tell Gore
that Clerke had died. Devotion to duty had been
the be-all and end-all of his existence.
An affable man, he was thirty-eight, had circled
the globe three times, and now advanced

within a few miles of Cook's record.
They were at the moment nearing the lighthouse
at the mouth of the bay of Avacha; when they anchored,
Gore, now Commodore, boarded the *Resolution*.
Ledyard was happy to look on Petropavlosk
and its surroundings in summer. What a change!
When they left in June buds were just tipping the branches.
This time grain had evicted snow; everything
growing was green; sleek cattle fattened
in the fields. As he had requested, Clerke
was buried on the south side of the bay, close
to the church at Paratunka, after palaver
with the local "pope." Ledyard and a group of marines
fired the last salute. Further, as Clerke
had planned, the ship's company enjoyed
a day off and a double allowance of grog.
Then the familiar round began again
of carpenters shaping sheathing for the battered bows
of the up-tilted ships, coopers making
casks, sail makers stitching sails,
sailors mending rigging, and all the rest
collecting greens, as Cook had prescribed
– wild celery, garlic, and spruce for brewing.
They weighed anchor; a merciless wind
pushed them eastward. One night
a flaming sky, "very awful," bespoke
a volcano (our Iwo Jima).
They bypassed Japan. Nevertheless
this wobbly path brought them safely down
to the South China Sea and the Portuguese port

of Macao, by the first of December. As they approached it,
Commodore Gore energetically carried out
the orders of the Admiralty; he and King
(now the *Discovery*'s captain) required all ranks
to deliver to them any journals, charts, jottings
or drawings -- any written document relating
to the voyage. King voiced his pleasure
in "their cheerful compliance," but the blow
fell hard on Ledyard. He had made
no secret of his desire to be appointed
historiographer of the voyage, earning the amusement
of a Briton like Burney, the novelist's brother.
But memory cannot be requisitioned. When a pilot
brought them into the estuary leading to Canton,
two English-speaking Chinese came aboard.
A shock of relief shook all of them
on returning to the world they belonged to.
For three years they could talk only in signs,
facial gestures, gymnastics of arms and legs
importing war and peace, trade and sex
in the lottery of experience and meaning.
To hear in the voice of strangers the very words
they had used all their born days
revived lost currents of emotion.
News flowed in: France at war with England,
the American Revolution still continuing.
Ledyard's American identity came to the fore.
He alone expressed no surprise
that his countrymen still held the British at bay.
But Gore's mind fastened on the French at war.

He had to protect his unarmed ships.
Up river to Canton, King went for cannon
and took with him skins of sea otter
to sell for the fabulous prices the Chinese would pay.
At Macao everyone basked in the wealth this booty
conferred. Corporal Ledyard exulted in luxuries
like the exotic cuisine of veal, pork,
duck, carrots, lemons, and spices that local
traders eagerly offered. Some of the crew
schemed mutiny, plotting return to the north
to exploit the fur trade. Not Ledyard.
Thoroughly loyal to the duty he had undertaken,
he never espoused the bitch-goddess success,
nor she him, in her beastly form
of money for money's sake. Yet the Yankee
in him warned that enterprise stemmed
from expectation of profit. The drama of his dream
would be to persuade someone to furnish a ship
for the fur trade, leaving him (once
he had guided them to its source) free
to cross the American continent alone.
After a month in Macao, the very name
Cape of Good Hope, mirrored their mood
as during late winter and early spring
they sought to leave the boundless Pacific waters,
its countless islands, mysterious human beings.
Thinking of them, Ledyard told himself
he was no scientist, able to solve their origin
but a friend to mankind and world citizen.
Time out at the Cape to repair the dangerous

fractured rudder on the *Resolution* and heal
those who came down with dysentery in Batavia.
They heard of the war with Spain, offsetting a response
of the decree by France that Cook's vessels be exempt
from attack in view of their priceless cargo of knowledge.
When the joyful sound "prepare to sail" rang out
with over a hundred live sheep on each ship
to sustain them, they entered the Atlantic in May.
Hoisted colors were friendly on the few vessels
they passed. Not so the loud-mouthed wind
shouting down the sails. They saw no land
for over three months, the longest time
during the whole voyage. The same vicious
blasts from the East blocked them from
sailing into the English Channel; strangely
they came to land at Stromness in the Orkneys
in late September. All the local gentlemen
came aboard to pay tribute to "the sublime
and soaring genius" of Cook; food was plentiful.
But they longed for English beef and beer, not to mention
a girl, a wife, or a mother. A few officers
went ahead to London. All others waited
for better weather by command of Commodore Gore,
"that conceited American." On their way
Sergeant Gibson died, the Marine who fell
overboard in Hawaii, the first to be rescued by
the newly invented life buoy. Promoted
Sergeant, Ledyard was twenty-nine as the *Resolution*
reached the Thames and their destination at Deptford
after four years and three months at sea.

With his pay in his pocket he stepped ashore
to begin his unpredictable itinerary.

He wrote in a letter to his mother, "I die
with anxiety to be on the back of the American
States, after having either come from
or penetrated to the Pacific Ocean.
The American Revolution invites us to
a thorough discovery of the continent. Let
a native explore its resources, draw
its boundaries. It is my wish to be that man."
When she read the letter, she said to herself
"I knew it." She had not seen her son
for years, not since the time when he
went AWOL from the British ship
moored in Long Island Sound. From there
he escaped to Hartford, where he wrote
his journal of Cook's voyage from memory.
Next he visited principal Atlantic ports,
Boston, New York, Philadelphia, seeking a merchant
sponsor for a voyage to the Northwest coast.
In the 1780's, the heyday of Americans in Paris,
his mother knew he lived at St. Germain.
He was proud he could walk to the capitol and back,
sometimes twice a day, the twenty-four miles.
There he met Lafayette, limping
from his wound at the Battle of Brandywine.
"Jefferson is like a brother," he wrote his cousin
with whom he regularly corresponded.
Some of Cook's glamor shone on him

in the eyes of others, like Madame Lafayette.
She borrowed his journal from Jefferson,
who was to become his lifelong friend.
He showed a lively interest in the plan
to return to the Northwest and helped
to find the means, even the chance
of a voyage there with John Paul Jones,
also a Parisian resident at that time.
As the lack of any available ship became clear,
a novel plan evolved in talks with Jefferson.
After a bizarre journey around the Baltic,
his aim was to cross the Russian Empire to Kamchatka
and there seek passage on a fur-trading ship
to his goal in Northwest America.
Before he left, the plan had been discussed in London.
The reception it met there bucked him up,
especially the backing of Sir Joseph Banks,
who had been the learned botanist of Cook's
first voyage and returned committed
to the study of geography and natural history.

Before he could start, he suffered a long delay
waiting for the required passport,
while Empress Catherine like Cleopatra
enjoyed voyaging in silk-curtained barges
down the Dnieper River, ambitious
to extend her empire into Turkey.
At last the passport arrived. By sheer luck
Ledyard got a lift to the eastward from
a Scottish physician traveling in Catherine's service

in a kibitka, expenses paid by the government.
From Moscow to Kazan on the Volga, then
across the Urals to Tobolsk, a city inhabited
by many exiles. The Scotch physician Brown
parted with Ledyard halfway across Russia,
about midway between St. Petersburg
and Okhotsk, still three thousand miles off.
Tumultuous rivers, skyward mountains
possessed the route to his magnetic goal.
Ledyard recorded differences of dress, color
and features of the people, writing
that color, I am now fully convinced
originates from natural causes and solely
from external and local circumstances.
He compared Tartars and Russians,
always apprising Jefferson of his observations.
He also described for him fossil specimens
he forwarded to the Russian scientist, Professor Pallas.
And with wry amusement he reported
that the tattoo marks on the back of his hands,
executed in the Society Islands, earned him here
the appellation of "wild man." In this remote
capital he was pleasantly surprised to hear
the health of Benjamin Franklin and that
of General Washington toasted enthusiastically
at the Governor's Table. This Governor
sponsored Ledyard's outward journey
with a courier carrying the mail. Freezing
nights, devastating winds did not
detract from the decency of the inhabitants,

who rarely accepted money for provisions
or shelter. Take the case of the woman
living alone who gave them enough
barley soup, onions, kvass,
and black bread for a hearty meal,
consenting only to accept one
kopeck – that was characteristic.
Reaching Irkutsk, Ledyard met
Jacobi, the Governor General, whose
power extended to the Pacific. Even
one so oddly and poorly attired as
this traveller now enjoyed the courtesy
of this venerable man. He soon
granted his permission to continue
with the courier. Delay in the preparation
of mail determined a halt here
in Irkutsk for a week. His heart
aimed like an arrow at the Pacific coast;
nevertheless in the interval he took
time to compare the native tribes
over which Russia ruled, seeing
physical and other traits of Kalmucks,
Buretti and Kamschadales, affirming
again his belief that variations
in colour and feature resulted, not
from design of the creator, but were
the outcome of circumstances. When at last,
free to travel again, he set off
by boat down the Lena River, reaching
Yakutsk after twenty-two days. He

had left Irkutsk at harvest time;
he got off the boat in September in
six inches of snow. As Governor
Jacobi had requested, the Commandant
of Yakutsk welcomed him, yet
strangely offered strong objections
to his plan to proceed to Okhotsk that
season. He (the Commandant) claimed
that weather caused such a venture
to be entirely impracticable, that ice
and snow made it too dangerous. Ledyard
chafed at the alleged barrier, no
stranger he to these conditions
— as if he had not encountered the Arctic!
The Commandant invoked the opinion
of a merchant who confirmed the assessment.
Without funds, and worst of all a virtual
unclad barebones, how could Ledyard
force the issue? Without the wherewithal
to resist, he felt condemned to
frustration, unable to enjoy the proffered
hospitality of being entertained by
the Commandant for months to come. *What,
alas, shall I do? By wintering here
I cannot resume my march until May.
I have but two long stages more,
when I shall be beyond the want
of funds, until emerging from
the wilderness I win the American Atlantic
States. And then thy glowing climate, Africa,*

explored, I will lay me down, and claim
my little portion of the fame for the globe that I
have viewed, with poverty as my fellow traveler.
Thus he soliloquized in his journal, projecting
his gaze on Africa now for the first time,
so far as we know – citizen of the world,
as he had characterized himself, and friend
to mankind. Next, an odd event
brought to Yakutsk a former
member of Cook's expedition, a Captain
Billings who was unqualified for
the task with which Catherine the Great had
had employed him on the say-so
of Professor Pallas. Billings, ordered
to explore and define the Northeast
Russian coast, had just returned
from the mouth of the Kolyma River to collect
other supplies. Ledyard, supposing
to be benefitted thereby,
chose to turn back with Billings to
Irkutsk. What could he have thought,
knowing as he did that Billings was
a fraud, no navigator? Well,
his former shipmate might have had it in
his power to transport Ledyard
back to America on that part of
the proposed new mission. On this
he gambled, in that far Siberian desert;
at least they spoke the same language,
had shared major experience. Though

in the pinch Billings failed to help; probably
no man could have. Then Ledyard
had been detained at Yakutsk, only
a few hundred miles from the Pacific.
Friendship with Billings might now
propel him there. In those days
a knock on the door at night was not
so ominously known as a signal
of disaster; but one February evening
Ledyard learned he was under arrest,
said to be a spy. He appealed
to Billings to clear his name; but the latter
refused to question what he called
an absolute order of the Empress. He
gave Ledyard a pelisse and a few
rubles. And Ledyard, stoical as ever
leaping into the kibitka, drove off
with his guards. Why did Catherine
the so-called Great (and she was so
in small ways, correspondent of both
Diderot and Voltaire, dreamer of small
reforms she would not put in effect,
a whore who paid her lovers
rather than being paid), why did she
have Ledyard hounded, hungry
and almost frozen, across thousands of miles
he had traversed as a friendly traveler?
Speculation's answer may be true, as transmitted
by Ledyard's biographer, Jared Sparks, later
President of Harvard. Weighing

available evidence, he asked
why Ledyard had been so long
detained at Irkutsk and Yakutsk? Sparks
supposed that the Governor and Commandant
acted in support of the Russian American
Company, which controlled the fur
trade with our Northwest, and refused
to have an American explorer gain
information about their methods,
especially their exploitation of American
Indians. The six months while
Ledyard had had to delay his progress
gave ample time for the Company to ask
Catherine to grant her intervention.
Her pretended concern, expressed to the French
Ambassador to rescue Ledyard from risk
in remote Pacific regions, she
herself refuted by the severity of his
treatment, as, ill and starving, he
was hustled to the Polish frontier,
told by his two guards if he ever
returned there, he would be hanged.
In one of the last entries in
his journal (which he had neither
will nor capacity to continue)
he lays down his earned conviction:
In the present state of privation, I have
a more exquisite sense of the immortal
nature of liberty than ever before. If every man
called to preside over the liberties of people

should once actually be deprived
of his own unjustly, it would qualify
him excellently. He would then be fonder
of it than any earthly possession. I could love
any country and its people, if it were
a land of freedom. I could condemn
with a better weapon than
St. Peter's those who deprive others
of their liberty or suffer any to
do so. A robust man,
his health when treated as a convict
had for the first time failed;
he now affirmed that regained
liberty. Rest among the beautiful
daughters of Israel in Poland had
restored him. To them let us
direct his celebrated eulogy of women
although written in Russia. "Women wherever
found are the same, civil, kind,
obliging, humane, tender beings.
They are ever inclined to be gay and cheerful,
amorous, and modest. They do not
hesitate as men do to
perform a generous act; not
haughty, not arrogant, but
full of courtesy, fond of society;
economical, ingenuous,
more liable to err than man,
but performing more good actions
than he. If hungry, dry,

or sick, or cold, or wet, woman
has ever been friendly to me; uniformly
so and her actions have been
performed in so kind a manner that
if I was dry I drank the draught
or if hungry ate a coarse meal
with a double relish." Thus his mind
in his thirty-eighth year. The question
at present confronting him was how
in his penniless state to pursue his way
back to England. When he got to Prussia
again, he thought of his patron, generous
Sir Joseph Banks, and drew a draft
upon him for five guineas. Enough.
Without hesitation he made haste
to London; in tatters approached Soho
Square and Sir Joseph's house, where he met
the trust he knew he could count on.
No sooner had he related his tale
of penetration of the Russian continent
than he found his beneficent patron had
more than mere relief to offer.
Banks told him of a task that would
test his utmost strength and commitment
to exploration: to undertake
an assignment by the newly created
African Society, which had assembled
for the aim of learning about the interior of
that continent. By the eighteenth century
men knew less of Africa probably

than the Greeks and Romans had; yet
the example of explorers, especially Cook,
set a high mark for their century,
which men must emulate in this blank
sector of the globe. Ledyard predictably
jumped at the chance. Banks sent
him on to Beaufoy, Quaker Secretary of
the African Society, the man primed
with details of this project
and in charge of the search
for someone to entrust it to.
He liked Ledyard at once,
the stamp of the man, broad-chested,
his resolute air and restless eye.
He noted too the unassuming
indifference to rank that betokened
faith in the equality of all men
rather than a slight to any. After
their talk Beaufoy asked Ledyard
when he could depart. The latter answered,
"Tomorrow." Well, the Secretary said,
it would take more time to prepare supplies
and instructions for the journey. Over
Ledyard's shoulder we may look
at his farewell letter to his mother.
Truly is it written that the ways of God
are past our ways of finding out
and his decrees unsearchable.
Is the Lord this great? So also
is He good. I am an instance of it.

I have sampled the world under my feet,
laughed at fear, derided hunger,
through millions of fierce savages,
over scorching deserts, the freezing north,
perennial ice, strong seas,
have passed without harm. What subjects
have I for praise, love and admiration!
After my travels of two years I am but just
returned to England and am going away
into Africa to examine that continent.
First I shall be in Egypt; after that
in unknown parts. Remember me
to my brothers and sisters. I pray to God
to bless and comfort you all, farewell!
I expect to be absent three years.
Thus he thought in June of 1788
when he left London, faring to France,
having agreed to move from Marseilles
to Alexandria, thence to Cairo.
Seven days of this then interminable trip
he allocated to Paris. He had to see
Jefferson who had suggested the crossing
of Russia, and endorsed the aim of connecting
west to east on the continent both belonged to,
becoming one when Jefferson sanctioned the Louisiana
Purchase. Now these two met once again;
Ledyard likewise looked up Lafayette.
An essay of friendship decorates the dialogue
between them, so apparently
unequal, honoring both. Ledyard

decided he detected a certain coolness
in Jefferson's manner; unmistakably
it was there; for his protégé
had re-entered the service of the British.
But what choice had he?
The new land offered no alternative.
He wrote his friend and cousin Isaac,
he could no more forget America than his God.
The one time would-be missionary rarely
resorted to religious language, voicing
his thought in the vocabulary of deism, like Jefferson.
Now he stood at the summit of his hope,
equipped well, his enterprise backed
by some of the keenest minds in England:
Banks, Hunter the biologist, Gibbon the historian.
Perishing no more in personal want,
he set out with material confidence
reinforced by the faith in the venture he always felt.
Having left Marseille, he arrived in Alexandria
after a slow voyage across the Mediterranean.
From his faithful reports to the African Society in London
we can follow his progress. "I left Alexandria
at midnight. Next morning at sunrise
I was at the mouth of the Nile." From the top of the mast
he viewed a great unbounded plain, "miserably
cultivated," yet supporting a multitude
of small villages in every direction. His boat
passed many others. He found a place
in the midst of its cargo, oblong melons, dates,
a horse, sheep, goats, a few camels,

a crowd of people listening to music in the morning
and the evening. Whenever they stopped at a village,
he walked with a Mohammedan among the mud huts.
Five days on the river refuted his reading.
"This is the mighty, the sovereign of rivers that
has been metaphored into one of the wonders
of the world? But let me be careful how I read
ancient history. A mere mud puddle,
rather than the reputed mystery of time."
It could not surpass the silk-blue Connecticut
or soft-flowing and word-bearing Thames.
But nothing deterred him from preparing for his journey.
In the confusion of Cairo "half as large as Paris"
and a hubbub of political confusion, he guessed, where
he did not know, what the unknowns were, and sought
the first round of information from Rosetti,
Venetian consul and British chargé d'affaires.
The line that Beaufoy had drawn on the map to the city
of Sennar led southward. Clad by Rosetti's advice
in Turkish garb for his own safety, Ledyard waited
three months in Cairo for a caravan to arrive
from Sennar and carry him along on its return.
A blaze of purpose impelled this explorer
to prepare thoroughly and without delay for his journey.
He strode through the narrow streets of Cairo
with their overhang of high buildings, ornate
mosque and mausoleum, minaret
with muezzin calling for protection to a prophet
glorifying war, nearby cloisters
of conflicting Christians claiming to interpret Christ.

"Religion," this reverend seeker wrote to Jefferson,
"does more mischief than all other things,"
repelled by so-called prophets and attempted
copyrights of a deity and by all who would exterminate
or exclude from benefits, wherever situated,
those who held opposing views. There
could be no religion, he held,
without accepting truth as universal.
Rosetti now informed him
twenty thousand slaves were sold in Cairo that year,
the majority of them women. He spent much time
with them, observing them chained ankle to ankle
by their black conqueror .
Trying to learn their language, he discovered
they had a word for slave but no word for liberty.
He reiterated to Jefferson the conclusion he
had earlier sent him from Russia after observing
various tribes of Tartars and Indians. Color,
he had concluded, resulted from circumstance not creation.
To him there was only one race, the human race,
to which we all belong without exception.
Reading these words, I hear Paul Robeson singing
"Black or white or tan
ain't the reason why
you can tell that man's
the purest kind of a guy."
He also visited in these markets the *jelabs*,
who are merchants who traveled to Sennar,
exchanging trinkets, soap, razors, scissors,
beads, and red cloth, for elephants'

tusks, Sennar gum, and slaves. The price
the king of Sennar demanded for his slaves
had to be paid in gold. After
the caravan finally arrived in Cairo,
there was a long delay in preparing for its return.
Chafing at this unexpected postponement of his start
on his major enterprise, Ledyard was stricken
with what proved to be his fatal illness.
Undiagnosed by local doctors, who
applied the wrong medication,
he died in Cairo before the caravan left.
Earlier he had written to Jefferson, "It would be
a consolation to think of you in my last hours."

Did he? Or was it R.E. of Stonington? with whom,
he wrote to his cousin, he had hoped to find "domestic bliss."
They used to meet in the woods above the pond.
The beauty of the pines reflected in daylight
on the water, knowing themselves to be
part of it, made them unite.
All life transcending memory, she
was inherent in all his ongoing future
and the start of his eulogy of women.
Lack of word from Ledyard worried Jefferson.
Lafayette, too, looked for news from London.
Tom Paine visiting there provided it.
The African Society reported without doubt
the death of Ledyard. "The man was all mind,"
Sir Joseph Banks declared.
He consciously lived his life like a story,

in which he was one of the characters.
What if he never made it to the sway-backed Niger
or crossed the American continent in either direction?
He had planted his hope in the generous mind
of Jefferson, realized by the Indian woman
who guided Lewis and Clark across the Rockies,
part of the story that is just beginning to unfold.
While in the far west, he never expected
to hear the silver chords of the hermit thrush,
until he listened to its newborn melody
as pure there as in his native New England,
and reaffirmed that the continent is one.
His distant gaze encompassing east and west
offers a self-discovery to all America,
where his mythos is enacted,
worthy to not remain so long untold.

SACAJAWEA

When they were about to move into winter quarters
near the Mandan villages, in what is now
North Dakota, Lewis and Clark first met her.
She came with another squaw to their camp; both
were wives of Charbonneau, the French trader
and candidate for the job of interpreter on
the next part of their journey. He was hired.
Sacajawea frequently visited the fort,
and they learned her story. She was a Shoshone
or Snake Indian, captured as a child of twelve
in a fight between her tribe and the Hidatsas
from whom Charbonneau had acquired her.
Now sixteen, she was pregnant; and the solicitous
Lewis partly acted as accoucheur,
giving her, on the advice of one of his men,
a rattle of the rattlesnake to swallow, to aid
her labor. The boy was christened Pomp
or first-born, in Shoshone, Jean Baptiste
in French. When the soldiers celebrated
their Christmas festival, she was there at the dance,
and at other times as the winter wore on.
Keeping in mind her knowledge of the Snakes,
from whom they needed to get horses to cross
the Rockies, Lewis and Clark decided, wisely,
to let her accompany her husband Charbonneau
and carry the child. When the ice broke up
in the Missouri, they resumed their upward voyage

against the current, some walking on shore,
others rowing or poling. Every day
the hunters searched for game, and soon
Sacajawea surprisingly added to their larder.
She would take a sharp stick and dig
in the earth, producing wild Jerusalem artichokes,
which she knew were stored underground
by the pocket rat, or gopher. Compared with her,
Charbonneau was feckless. One day when both
Lewis and Clark happened to be on shore,
the pirogue in which others sailed at the time
almost capsized in a sudden squall. Charbonneau,
at the helm, panicked and failed to steer her.
As the boat filled with water, indispensable instruments,
medicine, things for barter, floated out;
but quick-witted Sacajawea deftly fished them
out of the flood and caught nearly everything,
saving the fate of the expedition. We do not
hear how she cared for Pomp at the time, but he
survived, so she did that too. Perhaps
then Clark's high regard for her began.
Lewis carefully noted in his journal
"the fortitude and resolution of the Indian woman."
Three months after she joined the expedition,
now in its second year, she became very ill,
and such was Clark's respect for her, and recognition
of the need for her help among the Shoshone
that he devoted all his skill to her aid,
and Lewis wrote of his concern for "the poor
object herself, then with a young child

in her arms," she who was their main dependence
for negotiation with the Snakes. By the middle of June
1805 Sacajawea seemed likely to live,
and Lewis let her have broiled buffalo
well seasoned with pepper and salt, and soup
of the same, expressing "every rational hope
of her recovery." But Charbonneau, as usual
undependable, let her eat some white apples,
whatever they may have been, and she relapsed.
It was the end of the month before she improved
and showed it by going fishing. This
took place just before the major encounter
with the Great Falls of the Missouri River, when
the difficult portage of eighteen miles began
on rudimentary rollers made of cottonwood,
the only tree available there for the purpose.
They pulled their loaded canoes over ground
covered with cactus or prickly pear that drove
piercing thorns into their moccasins. One day
in a driving storm, a torrential flood came
down the creek they were following and almost
carried off Sacajawea. But Clark pushed her
with the baby up a hill, though she lost
all the child's clothing that she carried. As
they finished the footworn portage, they celebrated
July the Fourth. The captains allowed them
to finish the last of their supply of whiskey,
and they danced to the music of the violin, played
by Cruzatte, one of the soldiers. All this time
they missed seeing Indians. But by the end of July

Sacajawea at once recognized the land
where her people had traveled to get white earth
for paint, and more important to her fellows
she declared the forks of the Missouri to be
not far distant, raising the spirits of all.
Clark next went ahead by land, while Lewis
continued to pole upriver. They reached
the forks and named one for Jefferson,
and after much questioning, followed it
rather than the Madison or the Gallatin,
believing it would bring them closest to the Columbia.
One night, as they encamped, Sacajawea told them
this was the spot where the Snakes had their huts
when they were attacked by the Minnatarees, and
pursued as they retreated into the woods
with the subsequent killing of men and boys
and the capture of all the women. The next day
as they made their fire to cook an evening meal,
it was on the shore from which she'd fled into the river
and was overtaken. Oddly enough, they thought,
she showed no emotion in relating these facts
(that was to come later). "I believe,"
Lewis confided to his faithful journal, "if
she has enough to eat, also a few
trinkets to wear, she would be content anywhere."
But it was different when they met the Shoshone.
August came, and she marked a hill resembling
a beaver's head; from its shape she knew it
to be near the summer retreat of her tribe.
She assured her companions they would discover people

on this river, or on the one west of its source.
So great was their need of finding the Shoshone
that Lewis left Clark, who was lame, to stay
with most of the canoes and went ahead himself
in search of an Indian road. Exploring
various forks, he and his smaller party
reached the source of the Missouri and drank
from the icy fountain, feeling rewarded for all
the hardships of getting there. Their first meeting
with a single Shoshone Indian proved abortive.
Although Lewis, by using the Indian expression
"tabba bona," assured him that he was white
and made signs of peace, the native rode off.
Lewis followed the track he had taken
and a mile ahead met some Indian women,
of whom a young one took flight,
but an elderly woman and a girl failing to escape
sat on the ground and bowed their heads, expecting
to be killed. Lewis took them by the hand
and repeated, "Tabba bona," rolling up his sleeve
to show his white skin. Giving them beads,
mirrors, and some paint, he told his interpreter
to ask them to call back the girl who fled,
lest she alarm the Snakes and cause them to attack.
Upon her return he gave her also presents;
then, well coached by Sacajawea, he painted
the cheeks of all of them with vermilion, emblem
to the Shoshone of peace. Thus mollified,
the women led him as he had requested
to group of warriors ahead. How to enact

the rituals of diplomacy, lacking language?
Human nature prevailed on both sides
of the barrier. The Indians, after seeing the presents
Lewis had given to the women, embraced him.
Lewis then lit a pipe and dedicated it to them
and to London. In Russia, King wrote, "We met
but before smoking they all removed their moccasins,
a custom new to him. He then gave
extra presents, and they were especially pleased
by blue beads and vermilion paint. He explained
his friendly mission and handed a flag to the chief,
Cameawait, as a bond of union between them.
His gestured wish to go to their camp was granted.
In the leathern lodges, more smoking, more speeches.
And one of the Indians gave the half-starved Lewis
a roasted piece of salmon, the first he had seen,
proving that now he was near Pacific waters.

Meanwhile Sacajawea had stayed with Clark,
whose party slowly ascended this river,
and as she walked with him along the bank,
both just escaped being bitten by rattlesnakes.
Lewis endeavored to persuade the Shoshone
to take him and his companions to meet their colleagues.
But severe suspicion filled the Indian minds
that he was allied with their enemy, the Pahkees,
and only Cameawait with a few others would go.
Later, however, when it appeared that a deer
had been shot by one of the white men's hunters,
they all came up and hastily devoured it raw.

And Lewis gave them most of two other deer,
putting them in good humour. But when they reached
the river, not seeing Clark, their suspicions revived
and it was only by stratagems that Lewis kept them
from returning to their camp. Among other things,
he told them a Shoshone woman was with Clark,
also a black man, his servant York. Curiosity,
stimulated also by hope of gain, prevailed
temporarily. An Indian accompanied Drewyer
to look for Clark, who soon was found.
He had been walking on shore, as often, with
Sacajawea and Charbonneau, when suddenly
she began to dance, and sucked her fingers
to show that the Indians she saw were her own people.
And as the two groups converged, a touching
meeting took place, when first she recognized
a childhood friend who had been captured with her
but had later escaped from the Minnetaree. The women,
who had never expected to meet again, embraced,
renewing their friendship. While Sacajawea
talked with her friend, Clark went ahead
and was received by the chief, Cameawait,
who seated him on a white robe and tied shell ornaments
in his hair. In this tent of willows, moccasins off,
the smoking began, and the parley got underway.
Sacajawea, coming into the tent
and beginning to interpret for the white men,
recognized in the person of the chief, Cameawait,
her brother. She jumped up and hugged him,
threw her blanket over his head, and wept.

As she began interpreting again, she frequently
had to cry. When the council ended, she learned
that Cameawait and another (absent) brother
and her sister's son were the only living members
of all her family. She then adopted the child.
Before long the loaded canoes, dragged by
the exhausted soldiers, came into view. Now
they had the wherewithal to trade and more
presents to distribute. Instant surprise
overtook the Indians: Lewis's Newfoundland dog
and his air gun, Clark's servant York.
Could a man be black? They rubbed him
to make sure he wasn't covered with paint.
The whites finally got some horses, and Clark
set off to reconnoiter the Lemhi river,
which they mistook for the Columbus. Lewis
on August eighteenth made a birthday vow
to redouble his exertions and in the future
"to live for mankind, as I have hitherto
lived for myself." Sacajawea's brother
had diagrammed how the Lemhi river would
flow into the Salmon, and how then the Salmon
into the Snake, and the latter into the Columbia
which led to the Pacific or "Great Lake."
Clark's reconnaissance soon convinced him
that the Lehmi was not navigable, and therefore
more horses would be essential. But they lacked
articles the Shoshone would accept for barter.
Failing to provide enough blue beads,
they could only buy a few horses and a mule.

The plan was for the Indians to assist the whites
across the mountains. Before they set out,
they called a council of all the chiefs and warriors
and treated them to a meal of boiled corn and beans,
which was eaten with relish by the hungry Shoshone,
who had nothing to eat but a few fish. Cameawait
savored the dried squashes given to him,
better he said than anything he had tasted
except a bit of sugar that Sacajawea
had given him. He expressed a wish to live
in a country where they grew such good things.
The word came back that the white men
and their government would confer this power
upon him. Next day, Sacajawea learned that
the tribe intended to depart for buffalo country,
food being so scarce, and Charbonneau
incurred Lewis's wrath by delaying
for half a day before transmitting this
vital information. Lewis at once
reminded the chiefs that they had given
a solemn promise to assist them in transporting
their baggage across the mountains and that he
had divided with them the game that his hunters
had killed and promised he would continue
to share with them all that the white men had
to eat. The secondary chief said theirs was not
the decision to depart, and Cameawait,
after a silence, admitted he was responsible
for wishing to let his people go to the buffalo
hunting grounds, since they were in such need.

But he declared that having given his word
he would not violate it, and he countermanded
his earlier order. In all this parleying with him
Sacajawea interpreted, and it must have
made a difference that he was her brother.
They then resumed their march, the horses
and women carrying the load, the whites on foot,
but Sacajawea mounted on a horse
that Charbonneau had bought for her with articles
given by Clark, in effect a present from Clark.
Her child also rode on a horse, offered
by one of the Indians, so that he might direct
the advance of the party. Before leaving
the main body of the Shoshone, they bartered
for more horses. A typical price was one
of the battle axes made at Fort Mandan,
and a knife, a handkerchief, or shirt,
and a pair of leggings with some paint in addition.
Later the price went up, and they had to produce
pistols and powder. With an old man for a guide,
his four sons and another, they drove ahead
by what they thought was the shortest feasible route
to the headwaters of the Columbia river.
En route, deep sown snow, rain, sleet, rough
going, crossing the Bitterroot range.
They got more horses from the Outlashoot,
a new tribe speaking a guttural tongue.

Sacajawea undoubtedly could have stayed
with her own people, but she chose to follow

the Corps of Discovery, as Clark had named it,
with Charbonneau to the Pacific. Lewis
set down Shoshone marriage customs
in his journal, an exercise in anthropology
expected by Jefferson, and Lewis was good at it.
He wrote how the women in childhood were contracted
to men who were older, for a later marriage
arranged by the barter of horses and mules.
She had been thus disposed of,
and her original Snake husband, twice
her age, with two other wives, claimed her
when she arrived, but fortunately for her
he changed his mind because she had a child
by Charbonneau. Apparently her own opinion
was never asked; but she gave it herself
by staying with Charbonneau and the men of
the Corps of Discovery, and she shared
in all the hardships ahead, the hunger
and uncertainty, the indigestible meals, until
they reached a welcome prairie where roots grew
in the territory of a friendly tribe, the Nez Percé.
Here they left the horses, and carved canoes,
and after a party with square dancing to the fiddle,
they embarked at last on the Kooskooske River
and descended another on their way to the Columbia.
As they proceeded they encountered various tribes
in Indian lodges, conversing with them by signs.
We hear little of Sacajawea as the Corps of Discovery
navigated the various rivers, often portaging.
In one instance they let canoes down a cascade

with ropes of elk. She may have made them,
for on one occasion Lewis marveled greatly
that after they had eaten an elk she boiled the bones
and extracted tallow from them. Her principal value
now, however, was the evidence she brought
of their peaceful intentions. She, the journal
recorded, reconciled all the Indians they met
with the whites, since a party mainly of men
traveling with a woman and her child
could not be bent on war. In one place
where the Indians hid in their lodges, in fear,
the women wailing loudly, all came out
when Sacajawea and Pomp appeared before them.
Down the Snake and thence to the Columbia,
sometimes hitting submerged rocks in the river
and spilling their indispensable cargoes. Tribes
they met were friendly when not frightened, and
especially one chief, Yellepit, with a bold
and dignified countenance. As they neared the coast
they first saw geese, also a sea otter.
The Indians in this area knew some English,
which they learned from sailors trading with them.
Soon the Corps came to the last cascade
and had to unload all the canoes. They saw
a towering rock named Beacon on what is now
the Washington side of the river, several hundred
feet high, visible as a landmark for miles.

As they entered the estuary of the Columbia River,
fog, low visibility became the problem.

An Indian wearing a sailor's jacket here
volunteered to guide them down the channel.
This they accepted thankfully. As they neared
the mountainous country on the northern bank,
they heard the roar of the surf, and that night
they felt great joy as they camped, to greet
the long and sought for ocean.
At this point they were forty-one hundred
miles from their starting point at St. Louis,
probably a thousand from Sacajawea's and
Charbonneau's headquarters among the Mandans.
Throughout November the hunt for a camp site
was unsuccessful. Fog, rain, the treacherous
banks of the north shore were discouraging. Waves
flooding the dugouts on the land, floating tree
trunks, the shortage of firewood, all were obstacles.
Then, too, trade with the Indians languished
for lack of their favorite commodity, scarce blue
beads. They had not known enough to bring
more than a small supply. When Lewis and Clark
craved a sea otter robe, they got it only
when Sacajawea offered her blue bead belt.
The captains in return presented her with a coat
welcome in the wintry weather. Now it seemed
wiser perhaps to cross to the southern side
of the river. The question was put to a vote
and decided, Sacajawea planning to move away,
so she could find plenty of the plant wappatoo,
another one of her favorite edible roots
  — better fare for the nursing mother, surely,

than the horse meat and dog flesh she, like the others
had had to resort to. They hoped that on the south
side of the river they would also find more game.
Lewis searched for the winter campsite.
During his absence constant rain and gales
disconcerted the men and impeded their hunting.
Their clothes were rotted, and they had to repair
the old and make new ones out of the skins
they had saved. The diet of fish and berries
made many ill, and the hundreds of Indians
who visited them asked a higher price than they
could pay. At last the hunters brought in
some elk, and their spirits revived for a time.
Then Lewis returned, with news of a river
near which they might safely encamp that winter
with enough elk to subsist upon. They -
thereupon embarked in their canoes,
going continuously through the Columbia's waves,
and coasted around the bay they called, for Lewis,
"Meriwether," since he was the original
white man to explore it. They made their camp.
Clark left to find a place for making salt
and on this trip was greeted by the Clatsop,
Indians whom they considered neater and cleaner
than many others but madly addicted to gambling.
These were to become their neighbours, frequently
shrewd traders, for although files and fishhooks
were acceptable for some things, others cost
the blue beads they lacked. Heavy snow
dogged the efforts of the men to build their huts,

but the cold spurred them, and by Christmas eve
they at last moved in. After celebrating
with their scanty stores, they began to build
a stockade around the huts, and then forbade
Indians to come in between sunset and sunrise.
Sacajawea had her wish when they brought
bushels of wappatoo from the neighboring tribes.
She lived with her child and Charbonneau and several
other men in one of the huts. She
had given Clark two dozen weasel tails
for Christmas. To eat? They did eat tails
of the beaver; or maybe it was for the handsome fur.
(Unknown whether trapped by Charbonneau
or how they came into her possession.)
Illness among the men called on all
the resources of Lewis and Clark to minister to them.
But they set up the evaporation plant for salt,
which they had been missing. One day the Indians,
who had been watching the process, brought news
of a large whale stranded on the shore.
Sacajawea for once made a demand.
It would be a shame she said and hard for her
who had traveled all this way with them, if
she could not see the monstrous fish and look
at the Great Lake. Unlike the others she had not
been down to the ocean. Clark took her along.
But nothing was left of the stranded whale except
the startling skeleton; and all that they could accomplish
was to buy three hundred pounds of its blubber
– a lot to haul back to Fort Clatsop. We don't know

Sacajawea's opinion of the whale
or how she looked upon the broad Pacific.
The Corps of Discovery failed to see any ships,
and hope disappeared that they might reach home
in a sailing vessel – although one, in fact,
the *Lydia*, had spent a month in the estuary
of the Columbia, hidden from them by the fog.

After the probing winter, March and the smell
of thawing earth brought awareness of the time
to turn their faces eastward, and leave their visitors,
the Clatsop, Skilloots, and Wahkiacums, the last
of whom had been found thievish and impertinent.
Sacajawea did not comment on the squaws
of various tribes who came to the fort
offering themselves to the men. The Clatsop chief
was indignant when Lewis and Clark refused
the favor of his wife. They both warned
the men of the venereal disease that these squaws
had caught from the white traders on the coast.
The Killamuch tribe, who had welcomed them
when they went to see the whale, exacted
very high prices for the blubber they sold
and the few gallons of oil. Game had become
scarcer during the winter and harder to hunt.
Had it not been for the half-breed French-Canadian,
Drewyer, with his dexterous aim and his eye
to pursue a fleeing animal in the forest,
they would have fared worse, although all of them
now were expert riflemen. Having exhausted

their supply of candles, they molded new ones
of the tallow of the elk and used the skin for clothing.
At the end of March they turned Fort Clatsop over
to the Clatsop chief Coboway, who had been friendly,
and Sacajawea with them, they took their leave.
Paddling along the islands, they left the bay
and steered for the Columbia River. Creek by creek,
including Hungry Creek where they were hungry again,
and tribe by tribe, some new and some familiar,
some friendly and welcoming, others hostile,
the party ascended the Columbia, portaging often.
With difficulty they got a few horses from the Chopunnish
to carry at least some of the baggage. Wood
was so scarce that they had to buy some for fuel
and once they cut up a canoe for that purpose.
Thievery of their tomahawks and other
trading articles was serious, for they had so few,
and as a result could not buy any of even the last
year's dried fish. Their Chopunnish guide
assured them the nations higher up were friendlier.

They reached a hill from which they could see
snow-crowned Mount Hood. Without fuel
they shivered at night. As they progressed upstream
they saw some unusual native dancing. The Indians
all awaited the return of the salmon and danced
when the first swam up. Often at night
some of the horses broke loose and delayed their start.
All felt relieved when they reached the Wollawollahs
and the Chief Yellepit, who still prized the medal

they had presented to him on the way down. He
fed them and gave them wood, and gave to Clark
a fine white horse, receiving in exchange
a sword, one hundred balls, and some powder,
with which the generous chief was satisfied,
and he showed them a shorter route to the Kooskooske.

Among these Wollawollahs was a prisoner
who belonged to the Snakes, and by Sacajawea's
conversing with him, and his translating to his captors,
the whites could explain themselves better than usual
and answer the questions of the Indians, whom they treated
for various ailments, winning their confidence. At night
another tribe visited them, and the whites
danced to the violin; then the Indians danced;
and then they danced together. After this episode
they took their way again to the Kooskooske River,
and as they met other tribes, Clark bartered his skill
as physician for things they needed. Early in May
a chief of the Chopunnish – Bighorn they called him
because he wore a horn of the mountain sheep –
came to meet them accompanied by ten of his warriors,
an agreeable surprise. Later he joined them again
at a Chopunnish village, where only their medical skill
and their eyewater bought them food. They noted
further on the slim fare during the winter –
many Indians were forced to eat, for lack
of anything better, the moss that grew
on the pine trees. Now in May they were eating
the inner bark of these trees, though they also

managed to trap some trout. To them the whites
gave the entrails of a deer they had shot
and four embryo fawns. Later, on this route,
whom should they meet but the chief they called
the Twisted Hair, and Chopunnish, to whom they had
entrusted their horses on the way down, and who
also was to guard the cache of their saddles
in return for two guns and ammunition. He
received them coldly, to their dismay. Only
after they learned of his fight with another chief
were they able to recover the scattered horses again.
But their stay among the Chopunnish fortified
their rapport with the American natives, for
they learned to like several chiefs of that nation
who treated them with kindness and bargained fairly
and were cleanly in their persons and dwelling places.
Lewis and Clark went to unusual lengths to describe
the character of the United States to them.
Collecting all the chiefs and warriors together,
with a piece of coal they drew a map on a mat,
showing the relative location of their country.
They spoke in detail of its power and desire for
harmony among its red brethren and intention
to establish trading posts for their support.
This took half a day, for Lewis and Clark spoke
in English to Charbonneau, who then
relayed their meaning to Sacajawea in French.
She conveyed it to the Shoshone prisoner,
and he gave the gist of it to the Chopunnish, in
their own language, and so the powwow was lengthy,

and again Sacajawea was at the heart of it.
Next Lewis and Clark entertained them with
the wonders of their compass, magnet, spy glass,
and air gun. The son of one of the chiefs
presented them with a fine mare and her colt
as assurance that the council had cheered his heart.
At a following council the chiefs made a cooperative
reply and received presents from all the whites,
and various medical remedies they pleaded for
from Captain Clark, the most popular physician.
After further peaceful exchanges, the whites encamped
nearby to await the next full moon,
when, they were told, the snow would be melted
on the back of the Rocky Mountains they had to cross.
Here they feasted on bear meat, giving some
to their Indian visitors, who cooked it on pine boughs,
glad of the change from a vegetarian diet,
which the whites disliked, except when driven by
absolute hunger to eat of the berry cakes
and mush or soup made of edible roots.
For more than a month they lived near the Chopunnish,
waiting for tolerable weather to cross the mountains
and trying to amass food for the journey ahead
and present needs, with uneven success. So poor
at that time that they cut buttons off their clothing
to trade for roots, or made awls from a chain.
By the middle of June 1806, they were off for the Rockies
but confronted severe difficulty in finding a route,
until three Chopunnish consented to go with them
at least as far as the falls of the Missouri,

for the price of two guns. With their aid
they passed through the mountains. Then they formed
a bold plan to divide the party – Lewis
to return to the Great Falls of the Missouri,
then to explore the Marias River, while Clark
detoured far to the south, on the Yellowstone.
They took a risk, knowing well they might not
reconnect, but young, confident explorers,
they did not hesitate, determined to reunite
at the confluence of the Missouri and the Yellowstone.

Charbonneau and Sacajawea went with Clark.
He headed for the Beaverhead, and thence
by unknown routes for the Yellowstone. She,
Sacajawea, often reckoned the way.
As they were approaching the Continental divide
trails were too widely scattered to show the direction.
But she recognized the plain before them immediately
as one where her tribe had come to dig roots
of the camas, and she told her companions then
what creek they were on, and that as they reached
the higher part of the plain they would see a gap
in the mountains, with a high peak covered with snow.
And that is how they found Bozeman Pass,
later chosen by the Northern Pacific Railroad.
Clark named Sacajawea his mountain pilot.
Whenever she could she gathered vegetables,
wild carrots, fennel, gooseberries. Once
they came to a hot springs, and the men cooked meat
in the boiling water. This section of the route

brought them back to the place where they had formerly
cached their canoes, which now they relocated,
the men hardly waiting to unsaddle the horses
before dashing to find their supplies of tobacco,
their first good chew in months. From here
Clark and a flotilla of canoes went down the river,
and Sergeant Pryor rode overland with the horses.
Toward the end of July, Clark was on the Yellowstone,
which verified its name by its colour and beds
of stone and later of gravel. With the swift
current, Clark and his men floated rapidly
downstream, soon discovering a towering
two-hundred-foot rock, which he named
Pompey's Pillar. He climbed it for the view
and carved his name on the rock, as the Indians
before him had drawn animals and emblems on it.
Luckily game was plentiful in this region. They saw
some bighorns in their excursion up the river
of that name, and now on the Yellowstone buffalo
swam across the river in herds, blocking it
completely and impeding their progress. Elk
abounded, and beaver, so they were well supplied.
They made fast time, over seventy miles
a day. They met grizzly bears swimming in the river
and shot some in self-defense. Clark sent
a hunter for a specimen of the bighorn to the take home.

On August second they successfully reached the junction
of the Yellowstone with the Missouri, encamping
where they had camped more than a year before

in April 1805. Clouds of mosquitoes,
their all-too-frequent enemy, drove them out.
The face of Sacajawea's child swelled painfully,
and not awaiting Lewis, Clark moved
his company down the Missouri, leaving a note.
Sergeant Pryor arrived without the horses.
All of them had been stolen by the Indians,
and Ordway with his men descended the Yellowstone
after Clark, in canoes made from skins.
Now they scattered to hunt avidly
for other animals to trade their skins,
since they lacked horses as well as merchandise.
Sacajawea brought Clark a superbly flavored
gooseberry of crimson colour, and a species of currant,
which he gratefully enjoyed. With surprise at the event,
the party encountered two white men, hunters
from the Yellowstone, and from them they learned
of war between the Ricacas and the Mandan,
making it unlikely that they could persuade
some of these chiefs to return with them to the States,
as they had planned, likewise forestalling their effort
to establish peace between these tribes. Now Lewis
overtook Clark, undeceived by the fact that Pryor
had removed most of the note left at the confluence,
and reunited the Corps of Discovery. Lewis
was invisible, wounded the day before
by a shot from one of his men; but all were happy
to be together again as they attended him.
They soon embarked once more, and having the current
with them, and a strong wind, made eighty-six miles

before sunset. As a result they approached
the grand village of the Minetarees and fired
a blunderbuss to salute them as they passed.
They landed later at a village of the Mahahas,
or Shoe Indians, and from there crossed the river
to the Mandans, who warmly welcomed them back.
On the arrival of one their former Mandan interpreters,
Clark addressed the chiefs, inviting them
to accompany him to the United States and hear
in person the counsel of the Great Father, Jefferson.
But the principal chief of the Blackcat village whom
he attempted to persuade expressed a fear of the Sioux,
who had killed several of the Mandans since
their former visit. The Sioux were present
on the river below. With these friendly Mandans
Colter, one of the soldiers, wished to stay
and got permission and the pay due for his service.
Here, too, we take leave of Sacajawea
and Pomp, for this was Charbonneau's home.
In later years legends grew about her
among the Indians, some maintaining that she,
with an adopted son, traveled in the Southwest
and remarried, and accompanied Fremont for a while,
until she rejoined a tribe of the Shoshone.
But this remains hearsay, remote from the time.
What we actually know is that after the Corps
of Discovery safely returned to St. Louis,
Captain Clark adopted Jean Baptiste, or Pomp,
"my little dancing boy," writing Charbonneau
that he would take Pomp as soon as he was weaned

and raise and educate him like a son.
He also helped Charbonneau, offering him land,
or work as an interpreter,
all this in recognition of the woman
who, he said, had accompanied him so far
on the dangerous journey to the Pacific and back,
and who deserved a greater reward for her labors
on that route than he was able to give her
when at the Mandans. In a notebook of the 1820's,
he wrote that she had died. Since his word
serves better than the legend, let us leave her
in dignity where she was said to be buried then,
at Fort Manuel in the Mandans' territory,
where she and Lewis and Clark first met,
and look again at the statue of her I saw
in Portland, Oregon, as she stands today pointing
the route to the Pacific and the Ultimate West.
Her outstretched hand like a sensitive compass needle,
a signal that needs to be deciphered by
a new peoples' environmental Ledyard
searching for open space and the light of silence.

Laurence Stapleton was born in Holyoke, Massachusetts, on November 20, 1911. She was educated at Smith College and the University of London. In 1947-48 she held a Guggenheim Fellowship, and in 1972 she received a Fellowship in Creative Writing from the National Endowment for the Arts. Since 1934 she had been a member of the faculty of the English Department of Bryn Mawr College, where she retired as Mary E. Garrett Alumnae Professor Emeritus in 1980. She died in Bryn Mawr, Pennsylvania, on April 6, 1998.

Riverstone, A Press for Poetry

Riverstone publishes one award-winning chapbook of poems
each year. This is its first full-length publication.

Gia Hansbury, *Walking 14th Street Home* (1992)

Jefferson Carter, *Tough Love* (1993, out of print)

Marcia Hurlow, *Dangers of Travel* (1994)

Cathleen Calbert, *My Summer as a Bride* (1995)

Margo Stever, *Reading the Night Sky* (1996)

Gary Myers, *Lifetime Possessions* (1997)

Anita Barrows, *A Record* (1998)

Martha Modena Vertreace, *Dragon Lady: Tsukimi* (1999)

Laurence Stapleton, *Collected Poems* (1999)